SHIPWRECKS
OF
NORTH WALES

Ivor Wynne Jones

Landmark Publishing wish to thank the following for assistance in the production of this book:
Gwynedd Archives Service for the provision of additional photographs, especially Beverley Owen, who patiently dealt with numerous queries;
Andrew Morley and Helen Maurice-Jones for the provision of photographs and general assistance. It was Andrew (who runs Bay Bookshop in both Colwyn Bay and Rhos-on-Sea) who suggested the new edition in the first place.

SHIPWRECKS OF NORTH WALES

Ivor Wynne Jones

Landmark Publishing

To my wife
MARION JEANNETTE
the girl who sank a thousand ships – with her typewriter

Published by
Landmark Publishing Ltd,
Ashbourne Hall, Ashbourne, Derbyshire DE6 1EJ, England
Tel: (01335) 347349 Fax: (01335) 347303
e-mail: landmark@clara.net
web site: www.landmarkpublishing.co.uk

British Library Cataloguing in Publication Data

Jones, Ivor Wynne
Shipwrecks of North Wales.
1. Shipwrecks–Wales, North–History
I. Title
363. F2Y094291 DA740.N6

ISBN 1 84306 005 1

© Ivor Wynne Jones 1973, 1978, 1986, 2001

Fourth edition 2001

Printed in Great Britain by MPG Books Ltd, Bodmin, Cornwall
Editor: John Shouksmith
Design: Ashley J Emery
Cover: James Allsopp
Picture Research: Lindsey Porter

Front cover: The *Bobara* (p55)
Back cover: The *Marga*, Rhos-on-Sea,1991 (p143)
Page 3: The *Rethi Müller*, Penmaenmawr Beach (p103)

CONTENTS

'Wouldst thou,' – so the helmsman answered, –
'Learn the secret of the sea?
Only those who brave its dangers
Comprehend its mystery!'

The Galley of Count Arnaldos
H.W. Longfellow

LIST OF ILLUSTRATIONS

PLATES

LINE DRAWINGS IN THE TEXT

PREFACE
TO THE FOURTH EDITION

Three decades after the publication of the first edition it is difficult to envisage the maritime conditions that caused the tragedy and disaster this book seeks to unfold. Our earliest record of a shipwreck on this coast is found on a memorial stone of the XXth Legion, unearthed west of Roman Chester, and inscribed: OPTONIS AD SPEM ORDINUS C LVCILI INGENVI QVI NAVFRAGIO PERIT S E, which translates as "Optio in the century of Lucilius Ingenuus, awaiting promotion to centurion, who died in a shipwreck, is buried." A gap left for H (i.e. HIC, meaning "here") tells us his body was never found – the fate of countless thousands off the North Wales coast.

After two millennia of tragedy on these robust shores, shipwrecks are largely a thing of the past. The coaster has vanished from the little ports and natural harbours now full of smart cabin cruisers and pleasure yachts. Mersey traffic is but a trickle of ships equipped with the latest electronic navigational aids - although still obliged to take on a pilot at Point Lynas or the Mersey Bar. Most of our lighthouses still penetrate the dark with their reassuring beams, but all are unmanned, and the lantern of the once-famous Great Orme lighthouse is now a museum exhibit, returned to Llandudno after a sojourn at the offices of the old Mersey Docks and Harbour Board.

The popular passenger service between Llandudno and Douglas ended in 1982, when the Isle of Man Steam Packet Company surrendered to the motor car and switched to a roll-on-roll-off service to Heysham. Defence cuts have ended the once regular Royal Navy visits to Llandudno. Old piers are in a sorry state. The sea-going lifeboat has been withdrawn from Beaumaris, and replaced by a modern intermediate boat, larger than the inshore lifeboats that now do nearly all the work of the RNLI in these waters, aided by the rescue helicopters of 22 Squadron at RAF Valley.

The colourful pageant of shipping apparent when the first edition of this book was published in 1973 is now reduced to dinghies, wind-surfers, power boats, water skiers and swarms of noisy water-bikers, but nostalgia and public demand has made it necessary to bring out a fourth and much enlarged edition of what has long been the pioneering classic in its field.

Another element of today's affluence and availability of sophisticated equipment, is the increase in diving activity off the North Wales coast, much of it stimulated by the first three editions of this book (1973, 1978, 1986). Some of the resultant discoveries are set out in a new eleventh chapter written for this 21st century edition.

The memorial and grave at Holyhead for the
99 men who died aboard HMS Thetis, off
Llandudno, in 1939.

In 1700 a ship incongruously named the *Blessing* sailed out of the Mersey, successfully negotiated the North Wales coast and disappeared into the Irish Sea with a cargo of Lancashire junk. Several months later she reappeared at Liverpool laden with sugar, cotton and rum from the other side of the Atlantic. During her long voyage she had pioneered the infamous triangular trade via West Africa where the manufactured surplus of English sweated labour was bartered for black slaves – for the enrichment of the merchants of Liverpool and the peasants of Wales who harvested the shipwrecks which littered their coastline in proportion to the growth of the Atlantic traffic.

A remote nowhere in the sixteenth century and a primitive terminal for Ireland in the seventeenth, North Wales earned its own notoriety in the eighteenth and nineteenth centuries as a hazardous foreign land between Merseyside and America. Slavery was nothing new to the Cymry, the Welsh–speaking peasantry of Gwynedd, it was merely that the emphasis had shifted. In 1614 Cardiff-born Sir Thomas Button was appointed admiral of the king's ships in the Irish Sea with the specific task of guarding the coast against pirates. A veteran of the wars in the West Indies, Sir Thomas had taken the *Resolution* and *Discovery* into Hudson Bay in 1612 to try to ascertain the fate of Henry Hudson who had vanished while seeking the North West Passage. His task off the Welsh coast was scarcely less hazardous for the pattern of piracy had worsened with the arrival of the Arabs in search of white slaves. Writing from Holyhead in 1631, Sir Thomas said he had been chasing pirates – and even while he wrote 150 people were seized on the opposite shore to be sold into captivity in North Africa. In 1633 John Griffith, of Cefnamwlch, complained that a pirate ship had terrorised Pwllheli by entering the harbour and training her guns on the town while the crew carried out repairs. The truth of the matter was that Sir Thomas Button's title was more impressive than his fleet. Following the accession of James I, in 1603, the Tudor navy was reduced to a mere token force, and for twenty years Sir Thomas had to make do with a diminishing fleet of old and undermanned ships to guard a coast so remote that no one knows where he was buried after his death in 1634.

Charles I, who succeeded his father in 1625, recognised Britain's need for a strong navy and decided to create one with 'ship money' – the tax which eventually cost him his head. It was the Civil War of 1642/46, and the appearance of rival British navies in the Irish Sea, which rid the North Wales coast of pirates and paved the way for the commercial development of the Mersey. Great charter monopolies like the East India Company and the Levant Company controlled the best trade routes but the unfriendly Atlantic was open to anyone. Gradually the Liverpool shipowners discovered that for those able to survive the crossing with a leaking and overloaded vessel of 60 to 100 tons the rewards were enormous.

For better or for worse North Wales was geographically betrothed to Liverpool where, in order to obtain their first Dock Act in 1709, the city fathers argued that men-of-war lying in the open harbour were in constant danger of shipwreck. The resultant dock, completed in

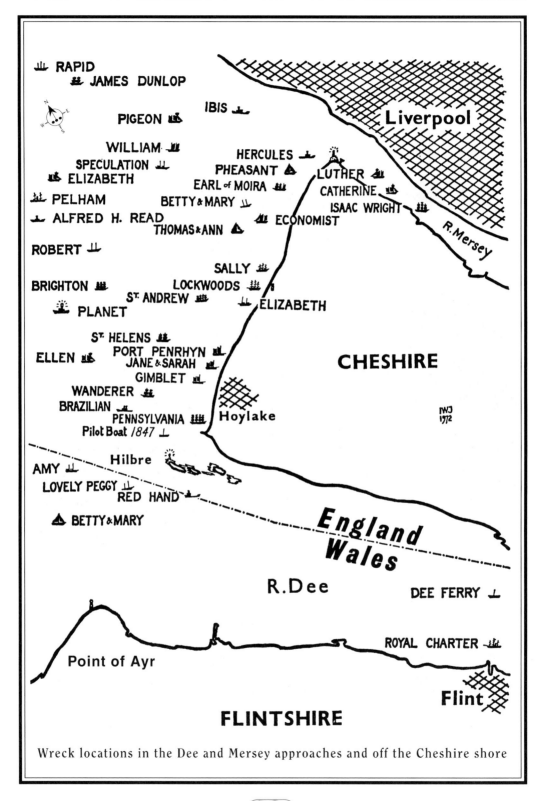

RAPID
JAMES DUNLOP

IBIS

PIGEON

Liverpool

WILLIAM
HERCULES
SPECULATION
PHEASANT
ELIZABETH
EARL of MOIRA
LUTHER
CATHERINE
PELHAM
BETTY & MARY
ISAAC WRIGHT
ALFRED H. READ
ECONOMIST
THOMAS & ANN

R. Mersey

ROBERT

SALLY

BRIGHTON
LOCKWOODS
ST. ANDREW
ELIZABETH
PLANET

CHESHIRE

ST. HELENS
ELLEN
PORT PENRHYN
JANE & SARAH
GIMBLET
WANDERER
BRAZILIAN
PENNSYLVANIA
Hoylake
Pilot Boat *1847*

IWJ
1972

Hilbre
AMY
LOVELY PEGGY
RED HAND

BETTY & MARY

England
Wales

R. Dee

DEE FERRY

ROYAL CHARTER

Point of Ayr

Flint

FLINTSHIRE

Wreck locations in the Dee and Mersey approaches and off the Cheshire shore

Coxswain Richard Evans, BEM and holder of two RNLI Gold Medal awards, takes the to sea for the last time, in January 1970.

1715, was a remarkable pioneering achievement for a town of only 10,000 inhabitants. It covered an area of less than four acres (on part of what is now Canning Place) but had no counterpart at Bristol creek whose western glory was soon to be eclipsed. By 1724 Liverpool Corporation had taken a leading role in improving the navigational safety of the North Wales coastal approaches, for in that year they authorised the use of 30 lb of gunpowder and £7 in cash to blow up some dangerous rocks between Anglesey and Puffin Island, at the eastern end of the Menai Strait.

In 1759 Capt William Hutchinson was appointed Liverpool dock master for the further expansion of the port. As well as providing Liverpool with its third dock (on the site of the present Royal Liver building), he introduced lighthouses and organised pilotage. The corporation and the port merchants shared the cost of promoting the first Liverpool Pilotage Act, of 1766, 'for the better regulation of pilots for the conducting of vessels into and out of the port of Liverpool.' The preamble to the Act stated: 'The entrance into the Port of Liverpool is very dangerous without a skilful pilot and many ships and lives have of late years been lost owing to negligence and ignorance of persons taking upon them to conduct ships into and out of the said port.' It became an offence to act as a pilot without a licence from a committee made up of representatives of the corporation, the merchants and master mariners. To qualify for the maximum fee, the pilot had to render his services from the Great Orme's Head, the scene of many a tragic wreck. The duty pilot cutter cruised between the Great Orme and Puffin Island in what would today be regarded as a somewhat hazardous pilot station. At the same time the committee prohibited the former (and present) practice of cruising off Point Lynas at the north-eastern tip of Anglesey. The western point at which compulsory pilotage should begin has been the cause of many an argument. German submarine activity closed the Point Lynas station during the 1914-18 War and the shipowners sought to make this a permanent arrangement. Again, in 1934, they sought an order abolishing the Point Lynas station and they were supported by the Mersey Docks & Harbour Board, but the Board of Trade rejected the application, saying that it would cause congestion and danger in certain weather conditions. Point Lynas pilot station was again closed during the 1939-45 War.

The shifting sands which were to close the Dee ports one by one also created navigational problems at the mouth of the Mersey. 'The entries into the harbour or port of Liverpool have been so dangerous and difficult that great numbers of strangers have frequently lost their lives for want of proper landmarks, buoys and directions,' said the Dock Act of 1709. Most ships then approached through a channel close to the Cheshire shore, relying upon what they could see by daylight. Paradoxically, North Wales could boast of a lighthouse, a coal-burning beacon built by private enterprise in 1716, on the Skerries, a group of tiny islands seven miles north of Holyhead. Under Capt Hutchinson, the Liverpool port authorities established lighthouses at the immediate approaches to the river and also at Point Lynas, Anglesey, in 1781 from which date the Point Lynas pilot station was re-established. The other lights established around the North Wales coast were Point of Ayr (1777), South Stack (1809), West Mouse beacon (1810), Rhoscolyn (1820), Bardsey Island (1821), Penmon (1837), Harry's Furlong beacon (1842), Llanddwyn (1846), Great Orme (1862) and St Tudwals (1877).

In conjunction with a lighthouse which Capt Hutchinson founded two miles inland at Bidston Hill, in 1771, ninety flag poles were installed in holes which can still be seen cut into the sandstone. There was a pole for each of the major Liverpool shipowners. As soon as a ship was identified in the approach channel at the mouth of the Dee, the appropriate house flag was hoisted at Bidston to give advance warning at Liverpool, three miles to the east. In 1827 this signalling system was supplemented by a sophisticated semaphore chain linking Holyhead and Liverpool through intermediate stations at Llanrhyddlad, Point Lynas, Puffin Island, Great Orme, Llysfaen, Llanasa and Bidston. By means of a simple system of two-digit codes covering most contingencies it was possible to send a message the seventy-six miles

Between-decks accommodation, typical of the overcrowded emigrant ships of the 1850s.

Britain's first named lifeboat, the Sisters Memorial being launched at Llandudno in 1861.

A North Wales casualty of the American Civil War: the Confederate Navy ship Lelia wrecked north of Prestatyn in 1865.

from Holyhead to Liverpool in less than half a minute – in clear weather – and it was by this means that many shipowners learnt that their vessels had come to grief almost within sight of home. The semaphore was used until 24 November 1860, when it was replaced by electric telegraph using the Morse code.

Geared to transatlantic trade, the development of Liverpool was checked by the outbreak of the American War of Independence in 1775, while the final abolition of the slave trade in British ships in 1807, and the Anglo-American War of 1812-14, added to the city's economic discomfiture.

Meanwhile the development of the steamship had been fostering new concepts of speed and reliability, despite an unpromising start. The first steamship to enter the Mersey was the *Elizabeth*. She arrived at St George's Dock on 28 June 1815, after an adventurous twenty - six days voyage from Port Glasgow, on the Clyde. The first steamer to visit North Wales was the *Cambria*, of Liverpool, a 90 ft long vessel which arrived at Bagillt, in the Dee Estuary, on 3 June 1821. By the following summer the paddle steamer *Albion* was maintaining a regular link between Liverpool and Bangor in the Menai Strait. It was to the Menai Strait, too, that the Isle of Man Steam Packet Co's *Mona's Isle* steamed for her maiden voyage in August 1830. A year later, on 18 August 1831, the Menai Strait was the scene of one of the earliest steamship disasters, the wreck of the *Rothsay Castle,* of Liverpool, with the loss of at least 107 lives (see Chapter Eight).

Although the Atlantic had been crossed by steamer as early as 1819, by the American PS *Savannah* – using sail for most of the twenty-eight day crossing to Liverpool – it was not until 1838 that the *Royal William* became the first transatlantic steamer to complete a crossing from Liverpool. Another five years were to elapse before the Admiralty invited tenders for the regular conveyance of mails by steamship between Britain and America. The challenge appealed to Samuel Cunard, of Halifax, Nova Scotia, who travelled to Britain to find two partners with whom he won the contract for two Liverpool-Halifax-Boston sailings a month. Four ships were specially built and the service commenced on 4 July 1840 – American Independence Day – when the *Britannia* sailed out of Liverpool under the imposing ownership of the British & North American Royal Mail Steam Packet Co. Blessed by the Admiralty, which had stipulated that the contract ships should be designed for fitting out as warships in an emergency, Samuel Cunard's enterprise was assured of success. For speed, safety and reliability one travelled Cunard, and to travel Cunard one went to Liverpool. By 1858 the Mersey Docks & Harbour Board had to be formed to cope with the rapid expansion and consolidation of Liverpool's role as the gateway to America.

In this role Liverpool was the port of embarkation for vast numbers of emigrants, thousands of whom were drowned in their quest for an American paradise. Apart from emigrant ships wrecked on the coast of North Wales, as detailed in the ensuing chapters, there were such disasters as that which befell the *Cataraqui* on 4 August 1845. She had left Liverpool fifteen weeks earlier with a crew of 54 and 369 emigrants, including 73 children, mostly from Bedfordshire, Staffordshire, Yorkshire and Nottingham. For the last four days of her voyage the weather had prevented Capt C. W. Finlay from taking any sights so that he believed himself to be sixty or seventy miles from land when the *Cataraqui* suddenly struck a reef near the entrance to the Hudson Straits. Darkness, driving rain and mountainous seas added to the confusion as the passengers tried to reach the deck. After about half an hour the ship rolled on to her side, immediately drowning about 200 passengers trapped below. At daybreak it was seen that some 200 survivors, including the captain, were still clinging to what was left of the ship. They hung on until the afternoon when the wreck parted amidships, reducing their number by half. As their second night of terror approached seventy survivors were counted on the forecastle, benumbed, hungry and thirsty. By dawn they were reduced to thirty and, as they continued to succumb one by one, the chief mate, Thomas Guthrie, seized a plank and struck out for the shore. He arrived to discover that a passenger, Solomon Brown, had miraculously been swept ashore alive during the night. Another seven seamen followed to make nine survivors who watched the final disappearance of the *Cataraqul* and the last of her 414 victims.

Sometimes the enemy was fire, as in the case of the 178 people who lost their lives aboard the *Ocean Monarch* (see Chapter Ten), or the 118 who went down with the Royal Mail Lines wooden paddler *Amazon* on her maiden voyage in January 1852. Another victim of fire was the American-owned *St George*, which left Liverpool on 24 November 1852 – carrying 127 emigrants and a crew of 25. She was found off Ireland by the *Orlando* which remained with her for thirty-six hours to rescue the crew and 76 of the passengers. Another American–owned emigrant ship, the *Mobile*, of 1,000 tons burthen, and nearly new, was lost with 60 lives when three days out of Liverpool in 1852. September of 1853 saw the disaster of the *Anna Jane* bound from Liverpool for Quebec with 500 emigrants. She struck Barra Island, in the Outer Hebrides, with the loss of 348 lives. The following month brought the loss of the *Isaac Wright*, off Cork, with many of the 610 emigrants who had boarded her at Liverpool. Another 297 emigrants were drowned when the 1,800-ton White Star ship *Tayleur* struck Lambay Island, North of Dublin, after leaving the Mersey in January 1854. Life was cheap and when the Liverpool vessel *Bona Dea* was dismasted in the Atlantic in January 1854, by a storm which also destroyed their food and water, the crew resorted to cannibalism, drawing lots to find the victim – a man named James Lilley. By the time they were found by the Sunderland vessel *Cuba*, most of the survivors were insane.

The appalling toll of the emigrant traffic gradually aroused the feelings of Welshmen on both sides of the Atlantic. At the Aberaeron Eisteddfod of 1873 the people of Cardigan Bay gathered to hear the winning poem on the subject of the sinking of the *Northfleet*, lost with 293 emigrants after being struck down by a hit-and-run steamer – an incident which produced the law requiring every British ship to carry her name on the stern and on both sides of the bows. A year later 'Drylliad yr *Atlantic*' (the wrecking of the *Atlantic)* was the subject for the principal competition at the Utica Eisteddfod, USA. This was in memory of the 546 emigrants lost when the White Star vessel *Atlantic* ran aground at the approaches to Halifax, Nova Scotia, in April 1873, while on her way to New York.

Amidst tragedy on such an enormous scale the North Wales coast proved to be one of the worst hazards of the Atlantic crossing. As steamships and navigational aids improved so the Welsh dangers diminished until 1914, and again in 1939, when German U-boats, joined in 1940 by bomber hordes from Brittany, endeavoured to sever the lifeline of the free world. It was from Liverpool that the Battle of the Atlantic was directed, with conspicuous success, enabling 143 million tons of shipping to reach the Mersey, and during nearly six years of war 3,500,000 British troops and 1,200,000 Americans passed through the port.

Defeated by the speed and efficiency of the modern airliner, Liverpool's traditional transatlantic passenger service ended in 1971, the year which also saw the demise of the 113-years-old Mersey Docks & Harbour Board. In a final bid to obtain extra revenue, the Board sponsored a controversial Bill which, had it become law, would have made their 1781 outpost of Point Lynas a physical extension of the Port of Liverpool for the unloading of super-tankers too big to reach the Mersey. However by the time the new Mersey Docks & Harbour Co took over the port and its problems, on 1 August 1971, Anglesey County Council had published a rival Marine Terminal Bill which was to receive Parliament's final blessing in October 1972, to secure the anticipated revenue for Wales. The Amlwch terminal has since closed but, as one sets out to tell the story of a thousand wrecks along the coast of North Wales, one wonders how long it will be before someone has the task of writing an appendix on the first super-tanker calamity in these hazardous waters.

CARDIGAN BAY

2

Open to the prevailing south-westerly winds, Cardigan Bay stretches for some sixty miles from St David's Head, on the Pembrokeshire coast, to Bardsey Island at the southern tip of Caernarvonshire. We are concerned here only with the northern half, commencing at the Dyfi Estuary which forms the convenient boundary between the old counties of Cardiganshire and Merioneth now Ceredigion and Gwynedd. 'Bardsey Island, being very high on the southern side, is the first land generally made in St George's Channel,' wrote William Morris, the hydrographer, in 1801, adding:

> It is allowed by most commanders of ships that if a lighthouse was erected thereon it would be the means of saving abundance of vessels that are constantly lost in the neighbourhood, owing to the causeway and the sand banks near the island, and it would be a good guide to the capital road of St Tudwal's.

William Morris was the son of Lewis Morris, the hydrographer responsible for the 1748 charts of the Welsh coast. When William Morris produced a revised edition in 1801 his advance subscribers included Capt Hugh Curren, of Philadelphia, Mr Atkinson, of the same port who ordered ten copies, and Mr R. Roberts, of Boston, with an order for fifteen. Other American mariners presumably relied upon their national motto ('In God We Trust') and charts which omitted the greatest hazard in the bay – St Patrick's Causeway, or Sarn Badrig in Welsh.

> Numbers of vessels have heen lost here owing, in great measure, to Captain Collins' chart which makes 10 and 17 fathoms in the very middle of it, when it is correctly ascertained to become dry the last quarter ebb; and he is too closely followed by all our mercenary chart contrivers, few of whom ever saw the places they pretend to describe.

Thus wrote William Morris. Bisecting the northern half of the bay, the Causeway extends for about eleven miles southwestward from Mochras point. South of it are the small harbours of Aberdyfi (Aberdovey) and Barmouth, while to the north one finds Porthmadog, Pwllheli and Abersoch together with the area known as St Tudwal's Road which provides good stiff clay anchorage and shelter from most winds.

The first of St Patrick's victims to which we can put a name was the *Caminhando*, a Portuguese ship of some considerable size which became trapped on the southern side of the Causeway early in March 1805. Her progress towards disaster was watched with interest by Capt Edward Roberts and his company of Barmouth Volunteers. This regiment had been raised and armed eleven months earlier for service in 'case of actual invasion or appearance of the enemy off the coast.' Upon joining, every volunteer would have been aware of the threat of the French repeating their 1797 invasion of Cardigan Bay (when 1,400 of the enemy

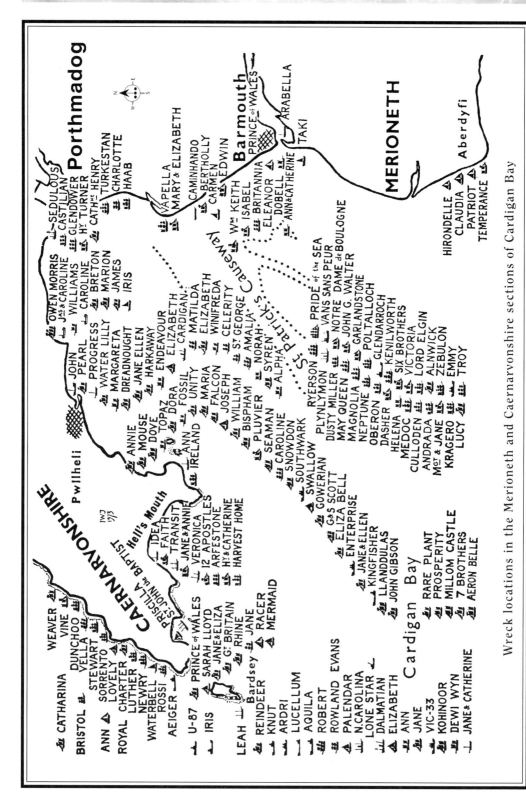

Wreck locations in the Merioneth and Caernarvonshire sections of Cardigan Bay

were rounded up by the Cardiganshire Militia, the Cardiff Militia and the Castle Martin Yeomanry in what was the last invasion of Britain). Whatever the thoughts of the Barmouth Volunteers as they watched this strange ship approaching their domain they were ready for her when she struck. More than that, the soldiers were able to salvage £6,000 worth of her cargo of corn, fruit and wine. In the face of such enthusiasm and efficiency one wonders why there were no survivors from the *Caminhando*. Was it a case of one lot of foreigners being very much like another to a local regiment warned to look out for Frenchmen?

'I never saw a place which presented so favourable an appearance, and that was at the same time so much dreaded by mariners,' wrote the Rev William Bingley in describing Hell's Mouth in his *North Wales* of 1801. Five miles across, these notorious jaws at the southern tip of Caernarvonshire have swallowed up more ships and human lives than anyone can ever calculate. 'None but strange vessels, even in the most boisterous weather, ever seek for shelter here, and when these are so unfortunate they are soon stranded,' added Bingley.

Geography was not the only hazard facing the sailor wrecked in Hell's Mouth for as Bingley's guide told him, aboard the Caernarfon cutter *Flora*: 'We remember more misfortunes to have happened in this bay and more inhumanity shown to the sufferers, than we have ever heard of anywhere else on the Welsh coast.'

Tales used to be told in these parts of a French ship, carrying many elegant men and women escaping from the guillotine of the Revolution. It was wrecked in Hell's Mouth and many of the passengers were swept ashore only to be attacked by peasants no better than the mobs of Paris. Without waiting to discover whether this human flotsam was alive or dead, the men and women of Lleyn stripped the bodies of their clothes and broke the fingers of the women to get at their jewellery. Such brutality was normal in an era when the dead and the dying were left naked on the beaches to feed the seagulls and crows. Not until 1808 did Parliament enact that bodies washed ashore were to be given a Christian burial.

The Bardsey light recommended by William Morris at the beginning of the century became effective in 1821 atop a 99ft tower built by Trinity House, to the design of Joseph Nelson. Bardsey Island lies a deceptive two miles off the southern tip of Caernarvonshire. The shortest navigable crossing is five miles, from Aberdaron to a cove two-thirds of the way down the eastern side of the island, and the earliest evidence of the hazards of this notorious crossing is to be found on a tombstone in Aberdaron churchyard:

> Underneath are interred the remains of Thomas Williams, of Bardsey Island, mariner, aged
> 49. He perished in the execution of his duty as Master of the Bardsey Light Tender which was
> wrecked on the 30 November, 1822. This stone was here placed, in testimony of his regard for
> the memory of departed zeal and integrity, by Joseph Goddard, Esq., Collector of HM Customs
> at Caernarfon, and Agent for the Bardsey Light. Also the remains of Sydney, daughter of the
> above Thomas Williams, aged 20, who lost her life on the same melancholy occasion.

There were six persons aboard the light tender that day and all were drowned to deplete an island community which then comprised about sixty people, living in twelve to fifteen houses built with stone taken from a thirteenth-century abbey. Another tombstone at Aberdaron tells us that John Williams, 40-year-old attendant on the Bardsey light, lost his life in crossing to the mainland on 14 April 1841.

Civilisation came gradually to the shores of Cardigan Bay. By 1824 there was a customs cutter at Pwllheli where, according to Richard Edwards, squire of Nanhoron, in a letter to the collector at Caernarfon, 'she is of as much use as if she was stationed at Charing Cross.' He was complaining about a schooner, ostensibly carrying a cargo of heifers from Guernsey to the Clyde, which had put into Hell's Mouth to unload smuggled silk, tea, brandy and gin. In the following year the newly formed National Institution for the Preservation of Life from

The Dutch brigantine Catharina was carrying salt from Runcorn for Riga when wrecked on Llandudno beach in 1869.

A large consignment of whisky intended for New Zealand was lost when the iron barque Stewart went ashore at Porthcolmon in 1901.

Shipwreck (now the RNLI) introduced gold and silver medals for gallantry and awarded one of the very first batch to Edmund Lewis, of Barmouth. Using ropes, and working alone from a dangerous cliff, he rescued seven of the crew of a vessel named the *Neptune*. Three years later, in 1828, Barmouth Harbour Trustees provided the port and the bay with its first lifeboat at a cost of £56.

The first recorded services of this lifeboat were on 12 September 1835. The master of the brig *Resolution*, on passage from Whitehaven to Cardiff, had put up distress signals after spotting the menacing turbulence which, at certain states of the tide, gives a hint of the presence of St Patrick's Causeway. The brig was still afloat when the lifeboat arrived and two Barmouth men were put aboard to pilot her to safety. Later the same day the barque *Zebulon*, bound from Liverpool to Quebec, struck the Causeway but with the lifeboat standing by she refloated on the rising tide, to return to Liverpool for repairs.

In 1837 the RNLI placed a lifeboat at Aberdyfi, the romantic little port known to every Welsh child. According to legend, incorporated in the song *Clychau Aberdyfi*, one can occasionally hear the church bells of the original town of this name submerged beneath the waters of Cardigan Bay. Many a pathetic tale has been woven at Aberdyfi, such as the tragedy which befell the local brigantine *Favorite* on 27 February 1839. With their ship anchored before the town, ready to sail the next day, the crew of four had arranged a farewell party with 17-year-old Ann Felix, daughter of the licensee of the Britannia Inn, and three girls

The auxiliary ketch Garlandstone safely moored at Barmouth after being refloated following a grounding off St. Patricks Causeway in 1968.

The Porthmadog schooner Owen Morris was almost home from Labrador, via Genoa, when blown into Black Rock cave, Morfa Bychan, in 1907.

from Mrs Scott's Boarding School for Young Ladies, at Penhelig. Owen Williams, John Angel and an apprentice named Lewis from Towyn, rowed ashore and met their guests at the Britannia where they lingered until 7.00 pm, waiting in vain for the fourth crewman, carpenter Edward Thomas. Eventually the party grew impatient and went out into the night.

Some hours later a worried Mrs Scott discovered that three of her girls were missing and her enquiries led first to the inn and then to the quayside from where a boat was despatched to the *Favorite*. When the brigantine was boarded she was found to be deserted, with a table neatly laid for a special occasion. Edward Thomas, the carpenter, was located on shore but could cast no light on the mystery for a troublesome horse had prevented his keeping the appointment. Neither could Capt Timothy offer any explanation for he had discreetly kept away from his ship while his crew prepared for another period of seaborne celibacy.

At daybreak the ship's boat was found wrecked at the mouth of the estuary. As the search was extended the tragedy unfolded. John Angel's body was found two miles away, on the beach below Foel Ynys, south of the Bar. Another mile to the south the body of Lewis the apprentice was found. The sea plays strange tricks for the body of one of the girls was swept two miles up the estuary to be deposited below her home at Tafolgraig. History has not recorded the resting place of two of the girls or of Owen Williams, the mate, but Ann Felix was buried at Towyn churchyard, some four miles to the north, beneath a verse composed by her father:

> Weep not for me, my parents dear,
> I am not dead, but sleeping here;
> Prepare, prepare to follow me
> You cannot prepare too soon;
> For the night did come
> Before I thought it noon.

A broken Mrs Scott died in the following year. The *Favorite,* built at Aberdyfi in 1804, survived the tragedy for seventeen years, until 5 December 1856, when, at about 10 o'clock at night, she was driven ashore in Dingle Bay, south-west Ireland, her master and crew being saved.

The storm of 13 January 1843, took a heavy toll of vessels on the western seaboard of Britain. Arriving off Barmouth with a load of coal, the Chester schooner *Edwin* took on the requisite pilot who then anchored her to await sufficient water to clear the Bar. There she was trapped when the wind increased to storm force. Dragging her anchor, the *Edwin* ran ashore half-a-mile north of the town and commenced to roll heavily among the breakers. Eventually one of her masts collapsed enabling four Barmouth master-mariners to use the accompanying tangle of ropes and canvas to climb aboard. By that time the pilot and five members of the crew were dead, lashed to the remaining rigging, but an apprentice who had been left to fend for himself was found alive, sheltering beneath a bulwark which had saved him from the suffocating blows of the waves and the chilling wind. The incident was forgotten until one March day in 1934 when, during exceptionally low tides, the remains of the *Edwin* were revealed. Her anchor chains were salvaged and a few links were mounted on a board to provide a relic for the Barmouth Sailors' Institute, founded on the quayside in 1890 by Canon Edward Hughes.

The same storm found the Pwllheli schooner *Mary & Elizabeth* at the southern end of Cardigan Bay. Rather than risk being dashed to pieces on the cliffs of Pembrokeshire the master put about and tried to return to the safety of St Tudwal's Road which he had left on the 12th. The schooner was within sight of safety when the wind veered and, in the effort of putting out the anchor, one of the crew collapsed and died. Within the hour the two remaining members of the crew also died, leaving the captain alone on board. When his anchor cable

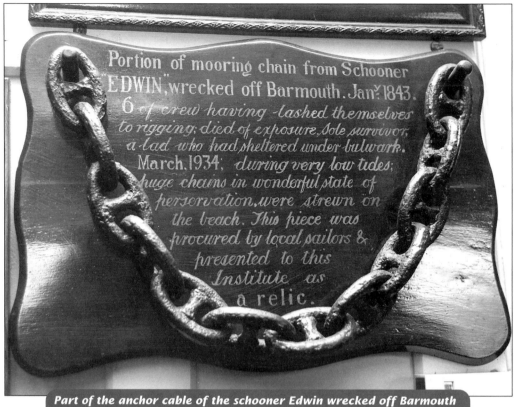

Part of the anchor cable of the schooner Edwin wrecked off Barmouth in 1843 and next revealed by an exceptionally low tide in 1934.

parted he lashed himself to the rigging and it was from there that he was rescued the following morning after his vessel had run ashore at Dyffryn, five miles north of Barmouth. Another victim of the storm was the schooner *Victoria,* of Barnstaple, which first struck the Causeway and then drifted off to finish as a twisted wreck on the beach near Barmouth. One body was found by the wreck and the rest of the crew were presumed lost on the Causeway. A Newport schooner, the *Bertholly,* laden with slates from Porthmadog, had left Cardigan Bay prior to the storm but was caught in the Irish Sea where she was dismasted. She, too, ended on the beach at Barmouth. One sailor leapt overboard and managed to reach the shore but nothing could be done for his shipmates until the storm abated, when the captain and two men were rescued from the rigging, a fifth man being found dead. At the northern end of the bay, the storm of 13 January wrecked three vessels at Abererch beach, a mile to the east of Pwllheli. They were the *Elizabeth*, a schooner laden with wheat for Liverpool, the Aberystwyth schooner *Water Lilly,* outward bound from Liverpool, and the Porthmadog smack *Margareta,* on passage from Amlwch to Swansea with a cargo of copper ore. All had been sheltering in St Tudwal's Road and had parted from their anchors.

Porthmadog's growing importance was highlighted by the wreck of the American ship *Glendower* on 20 July 1845. Porthmadog came into being quite fortuitously at the beginning of the last century after the construction of a mile-long embankment across the narrow neck of the Glaslyn Estuary. When William Alexander Madocks poured his money into the project his aim was to add 5,000 acres to his estate by reclaiming Traeth Mawr, a tidal basin which used to stretch to within 1½ miles of Beddgelert in the mountain fastnesses of Snowdonia. The re-routing of the river combined with the construction of lock gates to prevent the sea passing the embankment, resulted in a twice-daily scouring of a new deep channel around which the present harbour and town of Porthmadog were built between 1821 and 1824.

Simultaneously, the Holland family had started to exploit the vast slate deposits of Blaenau Ffestiniog and it was not long before a narrow-gauge railway was built along Madocks' embankment to link the quarry to the sea and make Porthmadog one of the busiest western ports. Porthmadog Bar, caused by drifting sands forever battling with the combined Glaslyn and Dwyryd rivers, presented a variable hazard at the entrance to the new port and it was here that the *Glendower* came to grief. Fifteen of her crew were rescued by what appears to have been a local pilot boat, a service which was rewarded with four RNLI silver medals.

Following the appointment of the Duke of Northumberland as president of the RNLI the whole of the lifeboat service was reviewed in 1851. It was ascertained that the Barmouth lifeboat was 'unserviceable and not worth repair,' and a lifeboat provided seven years earlier at Penrhyndu was completely discredited due to the frequency with which it capsized. Amidst this re-appraisal the Shipwrecked Fishermen & Mariners' Benevolent Society began to provide lifeboat stations in 1851, allocating one to Porthmadog. They used James Beeching's prize-winning design in the Duke of Northumberland's competition of that year and the boat was delivered to Caernarfon in October. However, when the Porthmadog crew went to collect her the lifeboat capsized in the Menai Strait and had to be towed upside down back to the harbour, the men being rescued by the *Caernarfon No 2* lifeboat and a boat from a nearby schooner. When righted and examined, it was found that two of the forward air cases were full of water and the boat remained at Caernarfon for some months for repairs.

Two brigs, the *Celerity* and the *Matilda,* were wrecked at Pwllheli in 1853 with the loss of both crews and, in December, the Penrhyndu lifeboat station was formally closed without having saved any lives. In 1854 the troublesome Porthmadog boat was replaced by one designed by James Peake and handed over to the RNLI who transferred it to Criccieth, thus bypassing the notorious Bar. Barmouth also had been supplied with a new lifeboat of Peake's pattern by the time the Baltimore clipper *Pride of the Sea* slammed into St Patrick's Causeway on 9 December 1854. Racing from New Orleans to Liverpool with a cargo of cotton, Capt Harp mistook Bardsey light for the east coast of Ireland and was under full canvas when his fine ship shuddered to a halt three miles off shore. Meanwhile the Liverpool ship *Culloden,* heading for home with a cargo of Canadian timber, had been following the clipper and also hit the Causeway, at the southern end. The crew abandoned ship and arrived at Barmouth in their own boats to give first news of the wreck. Later that night Capt Harp reboarded the *Pride of the Sea* to inspect the damage and take off food and blankets for his shipwrecked crew of thirty-six ashore at Barmouth. Next morning the clipper was seen to be on fire and she continued to burn for forty-eight hours before her hull collapsed.

A French brig, the *Charlotte,* of Le Havre, in ballast from the English Channel to Cardiff, struck the sand dunes near Harlech on Christmas Eve, 1855 – a remarkable example of hit-and-miss navigation in the days when a ship was entirely dependent upon winds. Having negotiated Land's End, she missed the 100-mile-wide mouth of the Bristol Channel and then swept the full length of Cardigan Bay. As soon as she struck the beach the crew of eight put off in the ship's boat, leaving the captain behind. However the boat overturned, plunging the men into the pounding surf. The drama had been witnessed by John Roberts, of Clogwyn, Harlech, who arrived on the beach in time to rescue four men – an act of bravery for which he was awarded the silver medal of the RNLI. Shortly before the *Charlotte* began to break up the master was taken off by Criccieth lifeboat.

Except for the endless permutations in human misery, there was a monotonous similarity to most of the wrecks on the Causeway. The *Plynlymon,* of Liverpool, carved a niche in

The schooner William, drawn soon after her launch at Porthdinllaen in 1839. She was wrecked at Porth Ysgaden, while sailing in ballast, on 9 October 1891.

The schooner Vine was built at Pwllheli in 1838. She was blown ashore at Porth Ysgaden in 1857.

The Norwegian timber ship Thora, aground at Porthmadog in 1929.

history on 9 March 1858, by being the first steamship to strike the hidden menace. All too often the victims were cotton ships like the *Troy*, of Boston, the *Britannia*, of Bath, Maine, the *Vapella*, of New Orleans, the *Ryerson*, of Yarmouth, Nova Scotia, or the *Kenilworth*, of Liverpool, with the raw material for the hungry mills of Lancashire. Sometimes they were sugar barques like the *Medoc*, of Bordeaux, bound for Liverpool from Havana, or the *Edward O'Brien*, of St Thomas, and the *May Queen*, homeward bound from Demerara, or perhaps timber ships like the *Castilian*, of London, returning from Quebec. Occasionally outward bound vessels, such as the Liverpool barque *Oberon* or the Oslo-fjord barque *Haab*, would be swept into the bay to end their days on the Causeway. Survivors of Liverpool-bound vessels repeatedly told of mistaking Bardsey light for somewhere on the opposite Irish shore, and in 1860 Trinity House introduced Cardigan Bay Lightship instead of the unlit buoy which, somewhat ineffectually, had marked the southern end of the Causeway since 1842. (The lightship was replaced by a lighted buoy in 1910.) In 1877 a further improvement was made by the erection of a lighthouse on St Tudwal's Island West.

When the Caernarfon flat *Ann* struck St Tudwal's Islands on 18 October 1858, her master could hardly have known that his humble little vessel was to become immortalised as 'Fflat Huw Puw' in five Welsh sea shanties. Capt Hugh Pugh was born at Liverpool in 1795 and his 60 ton smack-rigged flat was built at Frodsham four years later. In 1848 he sailed into Caernarfon where he settled down and re-registered the *Ann* – sometimes shown as the *Ann Pugh* – with the dimensions of 62ft long, 15ft beam and 7ft draught. On the voyage which carried her into immortality the *Ann* was doing nothing more romantic than carrying a cargo of timber for Barmouth and she might have been forgotten but for some unknown Welshman's love for poetry. Of his original words only one dramatic stanza survives:

> Fflat Huw Puw yn hwylio,
> Dafydd Jones yn rhiffio;
> Huw Puw wrth a llyw,
> Yn gweiddi Duw a'n helpo.

Losing everything in direct translation, these simple Welsh words convey a vivid picture of the *Ann* battling through Bardsey Sound, 63-year-old Capt Pugh struggling at the tiller and crying aloud for Divine assistance. During the 1880s Professor J. Glyn Davies spent many hours on the quaysides of Caernarvonshire and Liverpool rescuing the vanishing shanties of Welsh sailors, and often found that a good tune had outlived its words – in which case he filled the gaps so as to pass on a singable whole, thus giving Hugh Pugh's escapades a permanent home in songs which now resound through many a Welsh classroom. Hugh Pugh's son, Capt David Pugh, was master of a well-known Caernarfon schooner, the *Amity*.

Thomas Jones, born on Bardsey Island in 1877, has told of many a wreck forgotten on the mainland. He recalled a vessel laden with coal striking about a third of a mile north of the lighthouse. Like a gift from heaven, the coal lasted the islanders for many a year. The western cliffs of Bardsey have been claiming ships for at least 400 years and an enormous anchor of ancient vintage was found there towards the end of the 19th century. The Bibby Line screw steamer *Dalmatian*, 1,989 tons, built ten years earlier by Harland & Wolff, foundered in a storm near Bardsey in 1872. The Nefyn (Nevin) schooner *Reindeer*, of 97 tons, was abandoned off the island in 1874. The *Great Britain*, a Pwllheli schooner of 109 tons, was lost in the Sound in 1881. Another Pwllheli schooner, the *Jane and Eliza*, was lost there in 1885. Among the few names (and no dates) passed on by Thomas Jones was the *Leah*, of Scotland, which struck the western side of the island.

Llandudno's two centuries of copper mining history came to a symbolic end with the wrecking at Aberdaron in 1874 of the 34-ton sloop *Sarah Lloyd*. She was the first and last vessel to be built at Llandudno and was named after the wife of Capt David Lloyd who, in April 1861, swallowed the anchor to become the last lease-holder of the Llandudno mines. His 1862 output slumped to a miserable 100 tons but by that time his *Sarah Lloyd* was under construction beneath the south-western slopes of the Great Orme. Instead of carrying the anticipated copper ore to the smelters she was launched in 1863 to earn her living as a coastal tramp. Her loss added to Capt Lloyd's worries and he died in 1875, his widow finally surrendering the mining lease to the Bishop of Bangor in 1881.

The Rev Owen Williams, son of the founder of the Welsh lifeboat service (see Chapter Six) won a second service clasp to his RNLI silver medal when, as local secretary, he took Abersoch lifeboat to the *Dusty Miller*, a 596-ton barque straining at her anchors dangerously near the Causeway in October 1878. Despite a gale force wind the lifeboat stood by all night until a Porthmadog tug arrived to take the barque into St Tudwal's Road. The *Dusty Miller* survived to sail for many a year and her name appeared in the minutes of the Caernarfon Harbour Trustees as recently as November 1950, after a heavy oak beam rose to the surface within

Launched to the aid of two Porthmadog smacks, during a whole gale on 13 October 1910, the Criccieth lifeboat James and Caroline was first thrown on to boulders. After relaunching she was thrown on her beam ends, and became unmanageable, to be driven ashore and wrecked in the Dwyfor estuary, where she was declared unfit for repair. Her crew survived, as did the men aboard the two smacks, who were saved by Pwllheli lifeboat.

sight of the quayside. Capt Rees Thomas, the harbourmaster, said the recovered beam was almost certainly one which the master of the *Dusty Miller* had reported as lost overboard while discharging cargo at Caernarfon in November 1897. Built at New Brunswick in 1869, the Liverpool-registered *Dusty Miller* was owned by John Owen, of Ty Coch, Caernarfon.

Dynamite was never a very popular cargo and special precautions were taken when the Nefyn-built schooner *Sedulous,* of Porthmadog, was engaged to carry twenty tons of it to her home port in January 1882. The master was ordered to anchor in St Tudwal's Road and report his arrival to Porthmadog instead of proceeding to the normal pilot station outside the Bar. There she later took on her pilot and proceeded towards the Bar where, for many years, it had been the practice to accept a tow from a steam tug. As she neared the Bar, the crew of the *Sedulous* saw the duty tug leaving with another vessel, but the pilot decided that wind conditions were just right to catch the tide which would soon be on the turn. Having safely crossed the Bar, all on board were dismayed when the breeze suddenly faded, leaving the schooner in the grip of the ebb. Rapidly she drifted into the swirling quicksands where, after a few violent contortions, she broke up, the crew and pilot escaping in the ship's boat. As well as dynamite for Porthmadog, the *Sedulous* was carrying 150 tons of iron ore for Whitehaven. When the vessel disintegrated this heavy cargo gripped one of the masts which remained visible for more then half a century, and many a tale was woven around it for the ears of tourists arriving by train - the enemy which was to commit the Cardigan Bay ports to limbo. Quayside sages nodded their heads in November 1898, when Hell's Mouth swallowed the *Twelve Apostles*. Great symbolism was seen in this diabolical end to a fine old vessel which, with St Peter holding up the bowsprit, had become something of an unofficial flagship for Porthmadog. Even old St Patrick seemed to go into retirement, attracting only six clients for his Causeway during the

20th century: *Poltalloch*, a full-rigged ship of Victoria, BC (total wreck 3 January 1916); *John G. Walter*, schooner of Nova Scotia (refloated 9 March 1918); *Notre Dame de Boulogne*, a Breton ketch (14 September 1924); *Emmy*, a Greek steamer (5 February 1940, refloated after two days); *Vans Sans Peur*, a Breton trawler (25 March 1948, later towed off); and the *Garlandstone*, a 1909 auxiliary ketch (5 October 1968, refloated same day).

Weekend sailors have now revitalised the ancient harbours of a bay where recent wrecks have involved tragedies all the more poignant for the fact that the victims were amateurs – like the five schoolboys drowned off Criccieth on 6 September 1951. In the worst disaster of the century on this shore the fifteen people drowned did not even claim to be amateurs – they were holidaymakers who had embarked for an hour-long river trip aboard the *Prince of Wales*, of Barmouth, an ex-naval cutter which sank after hitting a pier on 22 July 1966. This far surpassed the nearest parallel tragedy, the loss of the pleasure boat *Arabella* on 1 August 1894, when ten members of a Bible study group were drowned.

A unique mishap! The hopper barge GKC 61 became stranded on her own load after discharging stone for the construction of Rhos-on-Sea breakwater in 1982. The stone had to be moved at low tide by mechanical diggers before she could be refloated.

CAERNARFON BAY: SOUTH

CAERNARVONSHIRE'S western seaboard is an inhospitable stretch of thirty-six miles broken only by Porthdinllaen, which offers good shelter from the prevailing winds although open to the north and east. 'The pier at Porthdinllaen which was begun to be raised by a gift of £600 from King George I, but never finished, is now almost in ruins, and if not looked after this excellent harbour will be quite destroyed,' wrote William Morris in his 1801 survey. Seven years later the Porthdinllaen Harbour Co promoted a Bill aimed at capturing the Irish mail-packet traffic but when Edmund Hyde Hall visited the port, to report upon developments beyond the original seven or eight cottages, he noted: 'There were half-a-dozen carpenters at work laying down the flooring of a new inn (the Whitehall); what was to be the new pier was already a sort of ruin, and the beneficial effects of the old one were said to have been materially abridged. Holyhead is in no danger of an immediate rivalship.'

Outward bound from Liverpool to the West Indies HMS *Ann*, a 14-gun frigate, was swept into Caernarfon Bay on 3 November 1760. 'All attempts to weather either Bardsey Island or Holyhead were fruitless. Therefore, on consulting with my officers, I was of opinion that the most prudent measure to take would be to run ashore on the most favourable sand beach that we could find, in order that as many lives as possible might be saved,' reported Capt Seth Houghton, adding:

> Accordingly we bore away, and passed Caernarfon Bar, which probably might have been attempted had we not seen the *Pearl*, a Liverpool ship, ashore there, where all the crew perished. Our ship struck a little after two in the afternoon about two miles to leeward to the Bar, and a quarter of a mile from the shore. Some of the people, partly by the boat, and partly by swimming, immediately got onshore, but I continued on board until near five, to persuade the remainder to attempt their own preservation. However, as they seemed obstinately determined in their resolution of continuing on board I then took leave of them and leapt off the weather forechains with my cork jacket.

Caught by a north-westerly wind, the *Ann* was wrecked at Dinas Dinlle, with the loss of eighteen of her crew of thirty-seven. The *Pearl* was wrecked on the South Sands of Caernarfon Bar. Fourteen bodies were washed ashore and buried in a common grave at Llandwrog.

At Belan Fort, at the mouth of the Menai Strait, there is a gun recovered from a full-rigged Spanish ship wrecked at Dinas Dinlle towards the end of the eighteenth century. 'There was great loss of life and treasure; I have often heard my father and mother speak of it. They drove down to see the place and witnessed the sad spectacle of numerous bodies, many of which, having been washed ashore near Clynnog, were laid on the churchyard green,' wrote Sir Llewelyn Turner who was mayor of Caernarfon during 1859-70. This wreck later brought about the ruin of a Llandwrog village tailor. Exploring the beach during a very low tide, he collected as many coins as he could carry from the vicinity of the old Spanish wreck.

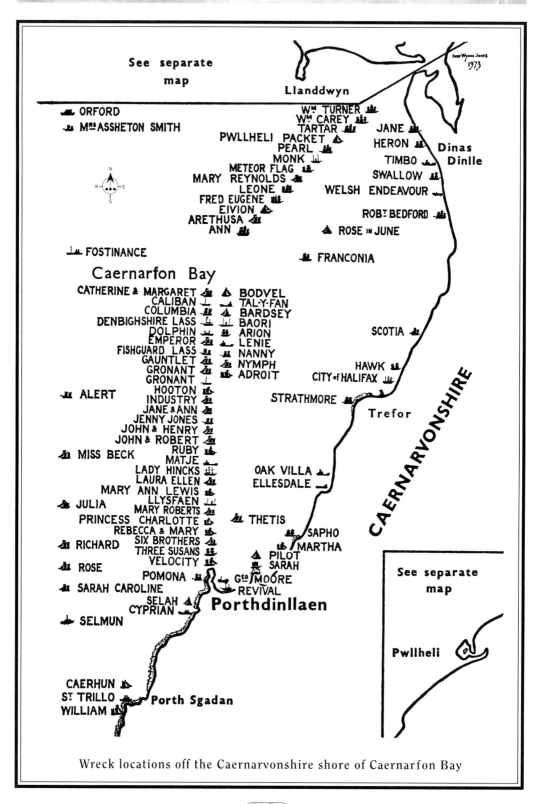

See separate map

Llanddwyn

Ivor Wynne Jones 1973

ORFORD
Mᴿ ASSHETON SMITH

Wᴹ TURNER
Wᴹ CAREY
TARTAR
PWLLHELI PACKET
PEARL
MONK
METEOR FLAG
MARY REYNOLDS
LEONE
FRED EUGENE
EIVION
ARETHUSA
ANN

JANE
HERON
TIMBO
SWALLOW
WELSH ENDEAVOUR

Dinas Dinlle

ROBᵀ BEDFORD

ROSE ɪɴ JUNE

FOSTINANCE

FRANCONIA

Caernarfon Bay

CATHERINE & MARGARET   BODVEL
CALIBAN   TAL-Y-FAN
COLUMBIA   BARDSEY
DENBIGHSHIRE LASS   BAORI
DOLPHIN   ARION
EMPEROR   LENIE
FISHGUARD LASS   NANNY
GAUNTLET   NYMPH
GRONANT   ADROIT
GRONANT
HOOTON
ALERT   INDUSTRY
JANE & ANN
JENNY JONES
JOHN & HENRY
JOHN & ROBERT
RUBY
MISS BECK   MATJE
LADY HINCKS
LAURA ELLEN
MARY ANN LEWIS
JULIA   LLYSFAEN
MARY ROBERTS
PRINCESS CHARLOTTE
REBECCA & MARY
RICHARD   SIX BROTHERS
THREE SUSANS
ROSE   VELOCITY
POMONA
SARAH CAROLINE
SELAH
CYPRIAN

SCOTIA

HAWK
CITY ᴏꜰ HALIFAX
STRATHMORE

Trefor

OAK VILLA
ELLESDALE

THETIS

SAPHO
MARTHA
PILOT
SARAH
Gᵗᵒ MOORE
REVIVAL

CAERNARVONSHIRE

Porthdinllaen

SELMUN

CAERHUN
Sᵀ TRILLO   **Porth Sgadan**
WILLIAM

See separate map

Pwllheli

Wreck locations off the Caernarvonshire shore of Caernarfon Bay

Abandoning his former industrious ways, he spent his ill-gotten fortune on drink and ended his days in the poorhouse. In the middle years of the last century another gun was recovered during a very low tide and was sold to Lord Newborough, of Glynllifon – who tested it with a disastrous effect on the windows of his mansion.

No longer restricted to low-tide exploration, marine archaeologists are slowly opening up the mysteries of the sea bed. In 1969 members of the Gwynedd branch of the British Sub-Aqua Club identified the remains of the *Lovely*, a 70-ton sloop wrecked 162 years earlier on Maen Mellt, a rock off Porth Newry, some four miles up the western tip of Caernarvonshire. After systematically mapping their find these amateur divers recovered thirty tusks, since identified as having been taken from immature African elephants, a quantity of copper sheeting bearing the imprint of Newton Lyons works at Holywell, and numerous 200 lb lead ingots originating at Eyton's foundry, Bagillt, Flintshire. They even recovered a copper hoop thought to have come from the cask of butter which the *Lovely* was known to be carrying. Some of these articles are now preserved at the National Museum of Wales, the remainder having been disposed of by the Receiver of Wreck who retained two-thirds of the value for the Crown, under the antiquated laws governing salvage.

In Affectionate Remembrance
OF
CAPT. ROBERT ELLIS,
OF THE
SCHOONER 'MARY REYNOLDS,' OF NEVIN;
ALSO,
WILLIAM ELLIS,
THE ABOVE'S ONLY AND BELOVED SON,
Who met with their death through drowning on the Carnarvon Bar, Sept. 26th, 1875,

Aged respectively, 52 & 17.
Interred at Nevin Cemetery, October 9th.

*Built at Nefyn, in 1846, the schooner **Mary Reynolds** was wrecked on Caernarfon Bar on 26 September 1875. The memorial card is for Captain Robert Ellis and his 17-years-old son.*

Porth Newry perpetuates the name of the 500-ton ship *Newry* wrecked here on 16 April 1830, when two days out from Warren Point, County Down, with 400 emigrants bound for Quebec. 'At the time the vessel struck the passengers were all in their berths, and most of them seasick. Upon perceiving their danger a dreadful scene of terror and confusion arose. Nearly all of them rushed upon deck with no other clothing except that in which they had laid down for the night,' reported an eyewitness. In an attempt to bridge the gap between his ship and the shore Capt Crosby ordered the mainmast to be cut down – only to see his entire crew, apart from the mate and one seaman named Hale, use this means to make their own escape without a thought for the passengers.

As the crew of the *Newry* vanished into the night a local sailor, David Griffiths, of Plas Bodafon, used this same makeshift bridge to board the stricken ship. During the next ten incredible hours 375 men, women and children were rescued by means of ropes and the mast and the exertions of Capt Crosby, the mate and Hale on the ship, and local men Owen James, Richard Griffith and John Pritchard on the cliffs, with David Griffiths alternating between ship and shore – an effort for which he was subsequently awarded the silver medal of the RNLI with £10 from Lloyds and a further £10 from the Underwriters' Committee of Liverpool.

After the terror of a night time scramble into the unknown or the horror of a daylight crossing of the chasm containing the bodies of some of the twenty-five who had fallen during the night, the survivors were faced with a 60-mile walk to Holyhead wearing little or no clothing and no shoes. Most of the emigrants arrived at Caernarfon on Sunday, 18 April - the day on which the *Newry* broke up without any of their meagre possessions having been salvaged. After a meal and four shillings (20p) each, out of a fund collected by Deputy Mayor William Roberts, they went on their way, sharing a further £37 collected at Bangor on the Monday. It was Friday before they left Holyhead aboard two Liverpool steamers, the *Satellite* and the *Abbey*.

When the brig *Sapho*, carrying a cargo of treacle from the West Indies for Liverpool, was driven into Caernarfon Bay before a westerly gale in 1839, the master, Capt Wallace, assembled his crew and gave each man two sovereigns which he ordered to be sewn into a safe pocket – to pay for their burial the next day. The captain and six of his men were duly buried in a common grave at Nefyn – the funeral having been arranged by the one survivor, an apprentice who was found on the beach sheltering in an empty treacle barrel.

Capt Hughes showed less foresight when he decided to slip through the Menai Strait while taking the wooden paddle-steamer *Monk* from Porthdinllaen to Liverpool on 7 January 1843. Leaking before she left and overloaded with 140 pigs and £600 worth of Welsh butter, together with the eighteen owners of the cargo and a crew of eight, she reached the hazardous Caernarfon Bar in failing light and on an ebbing tide. There was no safety margin when the steering gear developed a fault so that the *Monk* struck the North Bank. Hugh Jones, the engineer, and three of the passengers launched the punt in which they escaped. They alerted Llanddwyn lifeboat which took two survivors from the bows. The body of the foolhardy captain, surrounded by dead pigs, was washed ashore at Belan; the other nineteen victims were never found.

Most of the vessels which struck this shore soon became total wrecks. Among the exceptions was a Maltese brig, the *Heron,* beached a mile south of Clynnog in 1843. She was re-floated and towed into Caernarfon where she was dismantled and rebuilt as the Caernarfon brigantine *St Helen*. Launched in 1844, complete with her original figurehead in the form of a woman, the 144-ton *St Helen* was sold at Antwerp in 1852 and was removed from the register in 1883.

Another exception worthy of note was the ship *William Carey,* which, at 659 tons, was the second largest vessel ever built at Pwllheli. After the long haul from Calcutta, bound for Liverpool with a mixed cargo, she struck the South Bank of Caernarfon Bar on 12 February

Standard two-horse Board of Trade life-saving apparatus wagon as used on the Welsh coast until World War II.

The Oak Villa *at Porthdinllaen*

The City of Halifax *stranded at Llanaelhaiarn, 30 January 1872.*

1856. She was bumping badly in a strong south-west wind when Llanddwyn lifeboat got alongside her. Nineteen of the crew had been taken off when the ship suddenly refloated, leaving the master, the mate and one seaman still on board. As ship and lifeboat separated one of the Llanddwyn men – a Caernarfon Bar pilot – grabbed a rope and swung himself aboard the *William Carey*. With this skeleton crew she was sailed into Caernarfon and eventually completed her voyage to Liverpool. Built over a period of six years, she was launched in 1848 and vanished at sea in 1865.

Caernarfon Bay accounted for fourteen of the 223 vessels wrecked on the night of 25 October 1859, in what has come to be known as the *Royal Charter* storm (see Chapter Six). There were nine schooners at Porthor, a Spanish ship at Porth Colmon, a schooner at Tudweiliog, and two schooners and a flat at Porthdinllaen. Another schooner, the *Revival*, 96 tons, suffered the strange fate of being wrecked before she was launched – she was blown off her stocks at Porthdinllaen and had to be completed on the beach. She was re-registered at Liverpool in 1908 after being converted into a river barge and was broken up in 1916.

In 1863 the Receiver of Wreck reported that during the previous quarter century a staggering total of 206 ships had been wrecked within the Porthdinllaen area – a strong argument in favour of the lifeboat station established there in 1864. Porthdinllaen lifeboat saved ninety-one lives in thirty-three launches before attracting public attention, and then not for a rescue but for the crew's failure to go to the aid of the SS *Cyprian* – a shipwreck which was made the subject of a sermon at Westminster Abbey after it was learnt that the captain had sacrificed his life so that a stowaway might live.

Commanded by Capt John Alexander Strachan, the 940-ton (net) *Cyprian* driven by two compound engines developing 700hp, steamed out of Liverpool at 2.00 pm on Thursday, 13 October 1881, bound for Genoa. She ran into a north-westerly gale and when somewhere in Caernarfon Bay, late at night, the bottom tube of her starboard boiler burst. With the aid of the remaining engine Capt Strachan kept his ship bows-on to the storm until 8.30 am on the Friday when the steam steering-gear failed. In an incredible chain of misfortune a cogwheel then snapped in the hand-steering system, leaving the captain with no alternative but to lash the helm and rely entirely upon his one engine, until water entered the furnace depriving the *Cyprian* of all power. Capt Strachan had two more cards to play – his anchors – and when land was sighted at 3.00 pm he ordered soundings to be taken and dropped his port anchor in 15 fathoms. Failure to apply the windlass brake in time, resulted in the anchor running away with all its chain, and when the starboard anchor was dropped and the brake applied in good time, the chain snapped. It was then only a matter of time before the steamer struck the shore.

While checking the lifejackets of his crew Capt Strachan spotted a stranger – J. W. Klahn, a young stowaway who had emerged from his hide-out after realising he had chosen a doomed ship.

'No lifebelt, son?' enquired the captain, as he began to untie his own. 'Here you are, take mine, I'll swim for it,' were the last words he was heard to say. At 5.30 pm the ship struck about 250yd from the shore, two miles south-west of Porthdinllaen, and began to break up immediately. The stowaway was one of the eight survivors who were swept ashore alive, but Capt Strachan and eighteen of his crew were drowned. Capt Strachan's body was taken to Liverpool for burial and others were interred in an unmarked grave at Edern churchyard.

So much criticism was levelled at the Porthdinllaen lifeboat's failure to attempt a rescue that the RNLI took the unusual step of holding a public inquiry at Nefyn. Ten local master mariners declared the lifeboat could not have done anything for the *Cyprian*, and there was ample evidence to show that the vessel's strange behaviour, when first sighted off Nefyn, had led people on shore to believe she had been abandoned. Nevertheless Coxswain Hugh Davies had taken the precaution of calling out the coastguard life-saving apparatus crew who turned up with their rockets just in time to see the *Cyprian* break up.

In memory of Capt Strachan, a Mrs Noble of Henley-on-Thames donated £800 to the RNLI with instructions for a lifeboat to be placed on the Caernarvonshire coast. With this 37ft twelve-oar boat, appropriately named *Cyprian*, a new lifeboat station was opened at Trefor, eight miles north-east of Porthdinllaen, on 19 April 1883. The boat capsized, but without loss of life, on 12 December 1883, while trying to reach the Liverpool barque *Lady Hincks* which became a total loss. The station was closed in 1901.

By way of a postscript, Nefyn Parish Council honoured the unmarked grave at Edern with a memorial stone – 61 years after the tragedy. In 1968 amateur divers recovered the bell of the *Cyprian* from a heap of twisted metal not far beneath the surface.

Shore to ship line-throwing equipment officially described as life-saving apparatus, or LSA, until the 1960s change to 'coast rescue equipment' or CRE – was introduced to North Wales in the summer of 1815 after Parliament had debated the merits of Capt George Manby's invention. Resembling a large pop-gun, Manby's equipment comprised a mortar and a special cannon-ball with short chain attachment and a coil of rope. Duly impressed with an idea which had been shopped around since 1791, the House of Commons ordered the equipment to be placed at forty-five sites with particularly bad wreck records. Three of these sites were in North Wales: Point Lynas, Great Orme and Point of Air. Gradually the mortar was replaced by the more efficient rocket and by 1881 there were 195 LSA stations along the coasts of England and Wales.

Too late to be of assistance to the *Cyprian*, the Porthdinllaen LSA team were further disappointed a few months later when they exhausted all their rockets without establishing contact with the brig *Pomona*, of Dundalk, wrecked at Borthwen. With the sea breaking over the crew as they clung to the rigging, a coastguard tied a line around his waist and plunged into the sea. He succeeded where pyrotechnics had failed and it was not long before the breeches buoy was rigged up and all the men were got ashore.

Many unfamiliar dramas were played out in Caernarfon Bay after the collapse of France in 1940 and the German occupation of the aerodromes of Brittany. The twelve-years-old *Orford*, 19,900 tons, belonging to the Orient Steam Navigation Co, was bombed and wrecked in the bay on 20 August 1940. Her attacker, a Focke-Wulf Fw 200 *Kondor* of Kampfgeschwader 40, based on Bordeaux-Merignac, was damaged by RAF fighters and crash-landed in Eire. On 18 January 1941 the SS *Iris*, of Amsterdam, a 900 ton vessel of the Royal Netherlands Steamship Co, was machine-gunned off Bardsey Island. Her seriously wounded chief officer was put ashore at Porthdinllaen. Another Dutch steamer, the *Knut*, struck a mine and sank, her crew reaching Porthdinilaen in the ship's lifeboat. Yet another Dutch steamer, the *Aeiger*, struck a submerged rock off Bardsey and was abandoned, but with the Bardsey ferry standing by the vessel was reboarded and guided to Porthor where she was beached.

The saga of the *Lucellum*, a tanker bombed and abandoned off Bardsey on 19 December 1941, has become something of a legend in the world of fire-fighting and is commemorated by a model at the Fire Service College, Dorking. She was built at Copenhagen in 1938 and was registered at Liverpool with a deadweight carrying capacity of 14,580 tons, length 486ft and breadth 65ft. Owned by the Astrakhan Steamship Co, of Liverpool, she was managed by H. E. Moss & Co (Tankers) Ltd, of the same port, and it is to the latter that we are indebted for extracts from the ship's log describing the start of the drama. Laden with 13,474 tons (5 million gallons) of kerosene and light oil, the *Lucellum* left Belfast in convoy on 18 December. Next day she was attacked by a lone Dornier and hit by two bombs forward of the bridge, where First Officer W. P. Murray and Chief Engineer J. Rowntree were killed. With fires raging in the three forward tanks and the superstructure, Capt J. W. Swenson ordered his crew to abandon ship and thirty-seven of the original crew of forty-five reached Holyhead, one man dying ashore.

Two steamships aground at Porthdinllaen, the Matje (above) lost both anchors before drifting ashore; the Oak Villa (below) first ran aground at Porthnant and after being refloated was beached at Porthdinllaen.

The Oak Villa *being unloaded after being beached at Porthdinllaen.*

A Danish sailor took this photograph of the 14,580-ton tanker Lucellum *after she had been hit by two German bombs, off Bardsey Island, on 19 December 1941. She was abandoned but later reboarded by firemen and towed first to Holyhead, and later to Stanlow refinery.*

Meanwhile the abandoned wreck of the *Lucellum* continued to burn and, while making preparations to sink her, the Royal Navy also asked for professional advice from the National Fire Service which had been formed four months previously. At 10.15 pm Company Officer Jack Allen and six firemen put to sea in the Dutch naval trawler *Libra,* later to report that a fire-fighting operation was feasible provided sufficient men and equipment could be ferried to the drifting ship. Column Officer Leonard Loader, of Bangor, travelled to Holyhead for a middle-of-the-night conference with the senior naval officer. So as not to waste time, Mr R. Glynne Owen started to mobilise portable pumps at Bangor and at 9.30 am the first team left Holyhead aboard the Dutch tug *Zwarte Zee.* Mr T. A. Varley, chief regional fire officer of Wales, travelled from Cardiff to control the operation for which 200 firemen and twenty pumps were assembled.

Using an odd assortment of small naval craft, fifty-seven firemen put to sea, many of them boarding the tanker. The intensity of the heat under which they were working was such that a charge unloaded from the breech of the after gun exploded on the deck, causing a momentary fear that the German bombers had returned. By 21 December the fire was under control and the *Lucellum* was towed to Holyhead where she was left to cool off until 7 January 1942. She was then towed first to Liverpool and later to the Stanlow refineries where her remaining cargo was unloaded. On 15 January she was again towed across the Mersey, for repairs, and left Liverpool under her own power on 22 July bound for Londonderry, where she joined a convoy for Halifax, Nova Scotia. The *Lucellum* survived the rest of the war and was sold in August 1955 to a Norwegian company who renamed her *Asturia.* In 1958 her name was revived for a new *Lucellum* built by Cammell Laird for H. E. Moss & Co.

For this epic the North Wales National Fire Service were awarded two OBEs, one MBE, two BEMs and two mentions in despatches. After a long argument with the Admiralty, the NFS were awarded £1,000 salvage money in 1943, this being the first time in history for such an award to be made to the fire service. The money was shared among the fifty-seven firemen who fought the fire at sea. Using naval precedent, it was divided according to rank so that individual shares ranged from £144 1s 2d down to £7 4s 1d.

After the excitement of the 1940s the post-war scene has been somewhat quiet on this stretch of coast although 23 October 1963 produced an episode with all the ingredients for one of the classic wrecks of yore. It happened at Porth Sgadan where, at 4.15 am, the 314 ton MV *St Trillo* ran aground in a strong south-westerly wind. Launched in 1936 as the *St Silio,* and renamed in 1945, the *St Trillo* was the last survivor of the fleet of the Liverpool & North Wales Steamship Co, who catered for the needs of millions of holidaymakers between 1891 and 1962 when they went into voluntary liquidation. The *St Tudno* and *St Seiriol* were sold for breaking up but the *St Trillo* was bought by Townsend Brothers Ferries Ltd for their Cardiff subsidiary, P. & A. Campbell Ltd. It was while sailing from the Bristol Channel for her winter berth at Port Dinorwig, in the Menai Strait, that the *St Trillo* ran aground at Porth Sgadan.

'There was a terrible crash and I ran on deck in my nightdress,' said 21-years-old stewardess Miss Jean Carpenter, of Trafalgar Road, Cardiff, who was sailing with a crew of twelve men under Capt Owen Cecil Williams, of Bangor. The vessel was found to be fast by the bows and listing slightly to starboard. She was taking in water but the pumps were adequate and Capt Williams calculated that she stood a good chance of refloating on the rising tide within the ensuing four hours. To prepare for any eventualities, he asked the Porthdinllaen lifeboat to stand by at sea and the LSA team to be ready on the beach. Then, with coastguards lighting up the scene, he put Miss Carpenter and two stewards ashore by rope ladder.

Refloating at 8.00 am, the *St Trillo* was escorted by the lifeboat as far as Caernarfon Bar and then proceeded to the docks at Port Dinorwig where two small holes beneath the waterline were soon repaired. The next time the *St Trillo* hit the headlines was in 1968 when she was plastered

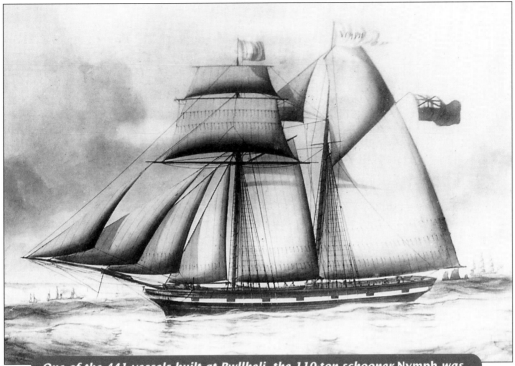

One of the 441 vessels built at Pwllheli, the 110-ton schooner Nymph was launched in 1839, and wrecked at Porthdinllaen on 4 November 1869.

The 400-ton MV Lenie, of Groningen, Holland, ran aground at Porth Ysgaden on 18 March 1964. She was able to pull herself off on the next flood tide, and proceed to Holyhead.

across the front pages of virtually every newspaper in the United States (see Chapter Nine).

Five months after the *St Trillo* incident a Dutch motor vessel, the 400-ton *Lenie*, of Steendam, ran aground in much the same position. Porthdinllaen lifeboat was launched at 5.30 am and by taking a rope from the stern of the vessel was able to haul her off on the flood tide. After being escorted for some five miles towards Holyhead the master of the *Lenie* reported that he did not need any further assistance.

A Caernarfon man's third attempt to emigrate to Australia in an ex-army amphibious DUKW named *Welsh Endeavour* ended at Dinas Dinlle on 23 December 1971. To a farewell cacophony of hooters from cars parked on the former Slate Quay, beneath Caernarfon Castle, the DUKW slipped her moorings in the old harbour and chugged out into the Menai Straits. The *Welsh Endeavour* was one of 21,247 DUKWs built in the United States between 1942 and 1945 to give the Allied armies a short-range ferry between ships and invasion beaches. It was designed to carry fifty-nine men or the equivalent in stores and was 36ft long and 8ft wide. After only five miles of her intended 12,000-mile journey, the *Welsh Endeavour* ran onto a sandbank and was wrecked in shallow water. For her owner, 32-year-old Mr Bill Parry, who had set out with one volunteer crewman, it was a bitter disappointment. On his first attempt at emigration in 1969 he had driven his DUKW deep into France before being forced to return to Caernarfon with engine trouble. On his second attempt he had been towed back from the English Channel. The letters DUKW, usually corrupted to 'duck' as an appropriate description of its amphibious role, were the works code of the original makers, the Yellow Truck & Coach Company, D signifying the year 1942, U for 'utility', K for 'all-wheel drive', and W meaning 'twin rear wheel axles.'

Five of the Rhoscolyn lifeboat crew were drowned during the seven hours they were at sea, trying to reach SS Timbo, of Whitby, straining at her anchors off Caernarfon Bar, eventually to be swept high up the beach at Dinas Dinlle, where four of the freighter's crew also lost their lives, on 3 December 1920.

ANGLESEY, isle of saints and sailors, provides Caernarfon Bay with its northern arm, an irregular harbourless shore of contrasts ranging from the former lair of the dreaded Crigyll outlaws at one end to the shrine of the patroness of Welsh lovers at the other. As recently as 30 October 1867 *The Times,* reporting upon the loss of the *Earl of Chester* noted: 'The wreck is now a prey to the notorious wreckers of the coast known to Welsh seafaring men as *lladron Crigyll* (the Crigyll robbers). Many hundreds of them were there yesterday stealing whatever they could carry away.'

One must go back another century and a half to find the earliest reference to the villains: 'On Tuesday 25 April, 1715, at the County Gaol, Beaumaris, were committed for felony three men, known as the *lladron creigiau Crigyll* (the robbers of Crigyll rocks), who were found guilty of plundering the wreck of the sloop called *The Charming Jenny* stranded at Crigyll.' The penalty for felony was death by hanging on the shores of the Menai Strait but Mr Justice Martyn caused a major scandal at Beaumaris Assizes in April 1741. Before him were Owen John Ambrose, of Llanfihangel-yn-Nhowyn, Gabriel Roberts, of Ceirchiog, Thomas Roberts, of Llanfaelog, and Hugh Griffith Hughes, also of Llanfaelog, all charged with robbing the stranded Liverpool brigantine *Loveday & Betty* which was driven ashore by a south-westerly gale on 31 December 1740.

Capt George Jackson, whose evidence is preserved in the great sessions records at the National Library of Wales, Aberystwyth, decided that his vessel could be saved with some assistance once the gale had abated. After tying up the *Loveday & Betty,* to prevent further damage, he set out overland to seek the customs officer at Aberffraw, five miles to the south. When the two men returned to the wreck they found the deck stripped of everything that was portable, including the sails and the 5in rope used to secure the vessel to the shore.

The capture of four of the robbers attracted considerable attention and among those who travelled across the island to Beaumaris, where the assizes were due to open in the quaint courtroom on 7 April, was William Bulkeley, of Bryndbu, Llanfechell (father-in-law of the Liverpool privateer Fortunatus Wright). Three days later the old squire noted in his diary: 'Tho this is the last day of the Sessions the Court sat to try causes till 3 in the evening; a thing never known before in the memory of man. Martyn the Judge being every day drunk deferred all business to the last, when they were hustled over in a very unbecoming manner.' In his drunken benevolence the judge discharged all the prisoners, causing Lewis Morris, the hydrographer, to write a poem deploring the fact that they had not been hanged – Morris had been employed since 1729 as searcher and customs officer for Holyhead and Beaumaris.

Anglesey justice had slipped even further into disrepute by 1778 when a corrupt jury was blamed for the discharge of several men accused of robbing a vessel believed to have been named the *Silcot.* Another victim of the Crigyll rocks, she rapidly fell apart, drowning most of the crew and the captain's wife, and spilling out a general cargo which was soon spirited away. Having failed in his prosecution at Beaumaris, the captain managed to bring some of

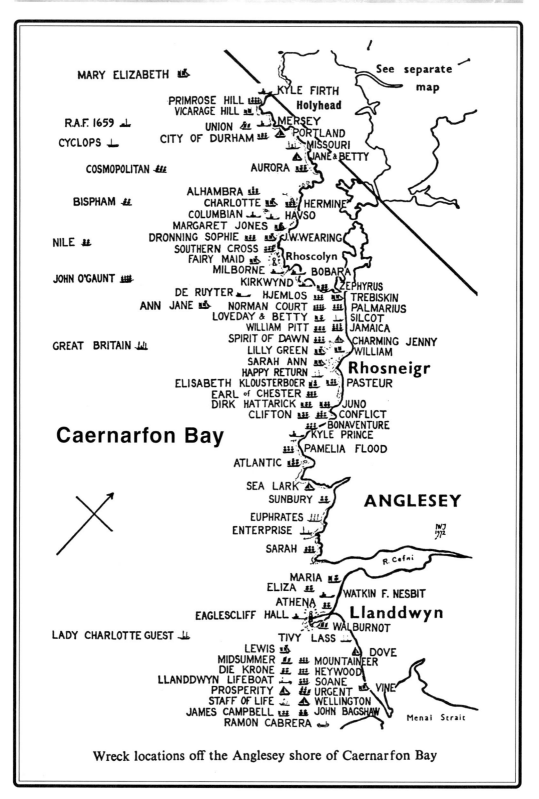

Wreck locations off the Anglesey shore of Caernarfon Bay

the men before Chester assizes where Siôn Parry, of Brynybar, was sentenced to death and the rest to transportation to the colonies for life.

Alarmed by the greed and cruelty of the peasantry, the Anglesey Druidical Society offered the then considerable sum of £10 in 1783 to any farmer who gave the greatest assistance with men and horses to save life from a wrecked vessel. While several decades were to elapse before the men of Crigyll ended their depredations, five men qualified for the Druidical Society's reward in 1809 by saving the crews of the *Happy Return* and the *William Pitt,* both wrecked on 6 June.

Reform was hampered by an unquenchable thirst for liquor. Bodedern parish records for 1815, noting the death of a 19-year-old youth, state: 'Owen Hughes died by excess of drinking rum out of a wreck. Inquest held on him.' Betsy's Cave, near Trearddur Bay, preserves the folk memory of another tragicomedy of the last century. At the back of the cave Betsy and her husband had built a store for such loot as might come their way from the multitude of wrecks which occurred here. One night Betsy, making good use of her specially designed skirts, made off with a haul of whisky while her husband busied himself helping the customs officers with their salvage work at Porth-y-Post. Only when he was satisfied that Betsy would have reached their hideout did the husband abandon his public-spirited exertions. On reaching the cave he found Betsy, unconscious with liquor, while a few yards away lay the body of their only son who had run away to sea and who had been swept home out of the wreck they had robbed.

In sharp contrast, nothing but good is known of the men of Llanddwyn at the southern end of this stretch of coast. An island during high tides and storms, Llanddwyn is joined to the mainland of Anglesey for most of the time. Here, in 1815, the Caernarfon harbour trustees set up a pilot station and built two cottages near the roofless remains of an ancient church dedicated to St Dwynwen, the Welsh rival to St Valentine. Much of the church appears to have gone into the subsequent building of a navigational beacon tower in 1819 and two more cottages and a bigger tower in 1845 – the latter being converted into a lighthouse in 1846. Appalled by the loss of life on Caernarfon Bar, at the western end of the Menai Strait, Admiral Crawley presented the harbour trustees with a lifeboat in 1825. In the following year this lifeboat was placed at Llanddwyn in a great humanitarian gesture which was of little practical value.

'She was kept at Llanddwyn with a few mats over her, winter and summer. I have often seen her when I was a small boy, with the mats blown off and a lot of sand lying in her,' wrote Sir Llewelyn Turner in his memoirs. Devoid of a slipway, launching carriage, or men to push her down the beach, and with only four pilots to row her, the lifeboat was never launched.

It was the loss of the schooner *Staff of Life* in 1833 which finally drew attention to the empty gesture of Llanddwyn. Watched by hundreds of people who gathered on Twthill, a natural vantage point near the centre of Caernarfon, the schooner broke up on the Bar with the loss of all hands. The harbour trustees then withdrew the lifeboat to Caernarfon.

Meanwhile shore-based life-saving apparatus was achieving some success around Holyhead, to the north, and the Rev James Williams, founder of the Anglesey Association for the Preservation of Life from Shipwreck, travelled to Aberffraw in time to heave a line across to the *Sarah,* a full-rigged ship outward bound from Liverpool, which was driven ashore on 7 October 1835. Shortly after the last of the crew of fourteen had been rescued the ship broke up. A cotton ship, the *Sunbury,* bound from New Orleans to Liverpool, was wrecked in the same place at much the same time, causing the Anglesey Association to query the value of a lifeboat at Caernarfon – where the advantage of an abundance of volunteers to man her was outweighed by the long haul out into the bay where most of the wrecks occurred.

Llanddwyn, it was argued, was a natural location for a lifeboat and, in 1840, the RNLI sold a Palmer-type six-oar boat to the Anglesey Association. Making use of a natural cleft in the

Wreckage of the 5,146-ton White Diamond steamer Missouri, of the Warren Line, may still be found in shallow water at Porth-y-Post, where she ran aground in 1886.

rock, the Caernarfon harbour trustees built a boathouse and ramp near the 1819 beacon tower. Additional crew volunteers were recruited from Newborough, three miles across the sand dunes, and the Llanddwyn pilots were equipped with a naval cannon to raise the alarm.

This cannon (which is still on the island) first boomed across the bay on 18 October 1841 when the Liverpool ship *Mountaineer,* returning home from South America, was seen to be rolling on the North Bank of Caernarfon Bar. Faced with a half-tide and gale-driven sea breaking on the Bar, Coxswain G. Griffiths decided to anchor his lifeboat and ease her in towards the ship by paying out cable. In this way he succeeded in taking off seventeen people, including the wife and three children of the master, a Capt Williams. There was only one casualty, a young boy who took to the rigging where he became entangled and was suffocated by the pounding of the waves breaking over the ship. For this rescue Coxswain Griffiths was awarded the silver medal of the RNLI and Sir Llewelyn Turner was presented with the ship's figurehead, a 6ft-high exquisitely-carved model of a Highlander which stood in the hallway of his home at Parkia, Caernarfon, well into the last century.

October was always a troublesome month for the Llanddwyn men. In October 1842 they guided the Exeter schooner *Elizabeth* to safety. A year later they did the same for the Waterford schooner *Liska* on the 30th and launched again on the 31st to the dismasted Cardiff schooner *Lady Charlotte Guest* which was later towed into Llanddwyn Bay by the Nefyn schooner *Maria Catherine.* October of 1846 brought the Liverpool ship *Heywood* into these troubled waters with a cargo of Canadian timber. The crew of twenty-two were taken off while she rolled badly on the North Bank but she was later refloated after the removal of her cargo. One of the lifeboatmen lost his life in 1846 while going to the aid of the Boston ship *Soane,* also stranded on the North Bank where all her masts snapped. After discharging some of her ballast, the *Soane* was kedged free and towed to Bangor to be repaired.

Many vessels were lost in Caernarfon Bay beyond the range of shore-based help. The Bibby Line lost two brigs in these waters, the Scarborough-built *Nile* in 1835 and the Liverpool-built *Bispham* in 1838. The *Cosmopolitan*, owned by Horsefall & Co, of Liverpool, was run down and sunk by the American ship *St Lawrence*, in August 1848. Both were outward bound from Liverpool and, apart from one man lost with the wreck, the rest of the crew of the *Cosmopolitan* were taken aboard the American ship and landed at Kingstown, which is now known as Dun Laoghaire, near Dublin.

A barnacle-encrusted wreck which appears from time to time among the shifting sands of Malltraeth beach, about a mile north of Llanddwyn, is still described locally as *y llong Groeg,* meaning 'the Greek ship.' She was the brig *Athena,* of Candia, which came to grief on 20 December 1852 while carrying beans from Alexandria for Liverpool. Having failed in repeated attempts to pull their lifeboat around the southern tip of Llanddwyn, the islanders recruited a team of horses from Newborough and hauled their 18cwt boat over the dunes to launch nearer the wreck, from which they saved fourteen men. Similar tenacity was shown by the Llanddwyn pilots six days later and again on the 27th. On 26 December they went out to the Prussian brig *Die Krone* on the North Bank and saved nine, while on the next day they rescued thirteen men from the Russian barque *Juno,* an effort which earned the RNLI thanks on vellum for Coxswain Hugh Williams.

The *John O' Gaunt* was the first of several China tea clippers to be lost on this shore. She was near the end of her voyage with a cargo valued at £30,000 when she ran ashore near Trearddur Bay with the loss of all hands on 16 January 1854. In the first fortnight of 1854 incessant gales caused the complete loss of 204 vessels on the shores of Britain. Several hundred more suffered serious damage. On 2 February the City of Dublin Steam Packet Co steamer *Fairy* offered her assistance to the Waterford brig *Eliza,* which was observed drifting off Llanddwyn with her sails torn and masts damaged. The offer was refused in the absence of the master, who had gone ashore to take a horse to Holyhead to hire a tug. With the *Fairy* still standing by, the *Eliza* struck a submerged rock west of Malltraeth and sank rapidly although the crew managed to get ashore. Nine days later the ship *Bonaventure,* bound from Savannah to Liverpool, was dismasted in the bay and driven ashore at Rhosneigr, where the crew all got away before the vessel broke up.

One of the many misadventures of the SS *Great Britain* occurred in Caernarfon Bay in 1854. It was her first voyage under the command of 34-year-old Capt. John Gray, the most famous of all her masters, who vanished through his cabin porthole while homeward-bound from Australia fourteen years later. On 28 April 1854 the *Great Britain* left Liverpool for Melbourne but soon after rounding Anglesey and entering Caernarfon Bay trouble was reported from the engine room. The *Illustrated London News* of 6 May reported that the breakdown was due to a burst steam pipe, adding: 'It is said that the accident will cause a detention of ten days.' Modern writers who have traced the history of the *Great Britain* attribute the ignominious return to Liverpool to screw 'damage' (K. T. Rowland, *The Great Britain*, Newton Abbot, 1971) or 'screw fittings deranged' (Grahame Farr, *The Steamship Great Britain*, Bristol, 1970). At any rate, it was 12 June 1854 before she again left Liverpool, carrying 450 adult passengers and 90 children, with £30,000 in gold sovereigns and half-sovereigns among her cargo. While she was at sea her ownership was transferred to the Liverpool & Australian Navigation Co who, two years later, were to lose the treasure ship *Royal Charter* on the shores of Anglesey.

Another ship built for the Australian trade, the *Southern Cross,* of Liverpool, became a total loss while sailing in ballast from London on 15 March 1855. She struck a submerged rock off Rhoscolyn Head and sank rapidly, although not before the crew of seventeen had all got away in the ship's boat. In darkness made worse by mist, the ship's boat also was wrecked on another rock just large enough to offer some kind of sanctuary to the men. It was twelve hours later before their plight was noticed from the shore and Rhoscolyn lifeboat was sent to their rescue – an operation requiring two daring trips through a rock-strewn sea.

Only two of the crew survived the wrecking of the American ship *Pamelia Flood* on rocks off Aberffraw on 20 January 1863. Eleven of the crew and a Llanddwyn pilot were drowned, the body of the master, Capt Anderson, being found beneath Ty Mawr, Clynnog. None survived the wrecking of the 493 ton Liverpool ship *Earl of Chester* when she struck the offshore rocks at Rhosneigr on 27 October 1867. Fourteen bodies, including the wife of the master, Capt W. B. Nancollis, were washed ashore and buried at Llanfaelog. Other members of the crew were never accounted for. 'For half a mile along the beach chests containing sailors' clothes, boxes with merchandise such as candles, wine and manufactured clothing, were scattered about,' reported *The Times*. This was the wreckage which was said to have attracted hundreds of the notorious Crigyll robbers but a private logbook kept by RNLI silver medallist Hugh Hughes gives details of 102 lives saved with the aid of his own fishing smack and a few Crigyll volunteers in the years before he was appointed coxswain of Rhoscolyn lifeboat. He gives no names but tells of twenty-four saved from an English ship in Cymyran Bay in 1866, ten from a Newfoundland brig in 1867, eight from a Spanish barque in Cymyran Bay and five from another Spanish barque at Porthygaran, and ten from an English schooner in Rhoscolyn Bay, all in 1870. His log continues with ten saved from a Newfoundland schooner in Rhoscolyn Bay in 1874, twenty from a full-rigged Spanish ship in Cymyran Bay in 1875 and fifteen from an English barque, also in Cymyran Bay, in 1881. Nevertheless, the international notoriety of the men of Crigyll was such that when John O. Williams, of the Rhosneigr coastguard, went

PELHAM JONES

Remains of the 855-ton clipper Norman Court *are still known to divers, half a mile off Cymyran beach, near Rhosneigr, where she sank on 29 March 1883. She won the tea race in 1872 with a voyage of 96 days from China. She had been re-rigged as a barque and was carrying sugar from Java on her last voyage.*

A helicopter of the RAF's North Wales rescue service, based on Rhosneigr, seen over Pilots Cove and the derelict lifeboat house at Llanddwyn.

out to a stranded French barque-rigged steamer in 1878 the officers used their revolvers to keep him at bay. This was the year in which a deputation of Rhosneigr men turned up at an inspection by Admiral Sir Augustus Phillimore, admiral-superintendent of naval reserves, to complain that Mr Williams was taking away their living by warning vessels out of the bay with rockets.

To the south, the men of Llanddwyn were kept busy. The *Maria*, an Amlwch brigantine was wrecked near the island on 3 December 1863, the crew of four being saved; the *James Campbell*, a barque of Nova Scotia, broke up on the North Bank on 21 October 1867, the crew of eleven escaping in their own boat and later transferring to the lifeboat; there was no one to be saved when the capsized ship *Euphrates* was washed ashore at Aberffraw in December 1867. Coastguards rescued the crew of the barque *Atlantic* when she was driven on to rocks off Aberffraw in January 1868. The *Dove*, a Pwllheli sloop, was wrecked on Newborough beach in 1869; the *John Bagshaw*, a brig, was wrecked on the North Bank in February 1870, some of the crew getting away in their own boat; the same month saw the loss of the Caernarfon schooner *Lewis*, off Llanddwyn, and the abandonment of another Caernarfon schooner, the *Scotia*, which was later boarded and salvaged by the Porthdinllaen lifeboat crew.

The pilots and lifeboatmen of Llanddwyn were one and the same, so that it was a major disaster when four pilots and two apprentices were drowned on 24 January 1874. The pilot boat had left the island in the afternoon to take off the man who was piloting the schooner *Margaret* out of Caernarfon. They were last seen alongside the schooner west of Caernarfon Bar in a strong west-north-westerly wind. The body of one of the pilots was washed ashore near Caernarfon later that night and their upturned boat came ashore near Dinas Dinlle.

A lifeboat station was established at Rhosneigr in 1872, their first rescue launch being to the Liverpool barque *Clifton* on 3 January 1876, when ten men were saved. After losing her foremast while returning home with a cargo of cotton and sugar, the barque drifted on to Crigyll rocks. Their next launch was on 1 March 1878 when the Dutch brigantine *Elisabeth Kloust-erboer* ended her days on the same notorious reef. The drama had begun at about 3.00 am when Coastguard Williams took an armful of rockets down to the beach. It was not long before he saw a dim port-side light where no vessel ought to have been and fired off two rockets, causing the light to disappear to sea. Some time later he warned a steamer in the same way and later still endeavoured to warn yet a third vessel – the *Elisabeth Klousterboer* – which reacted immediately but had insufficient space in which to manoeuvre. Williams heard the groan of breaking timber as the brigantine struck and he called out the lifeboat. There was one survivor, the helmsman Jacob Biering, who was found clinging to a small rock a quarter of a mile away. He said that the brigantine was also the first vessel warned off by Williams but

This 6ft high figurehead from the Liverpool ship **Mountaineer** *stood in the hallway of Parkia, the Caernarfon home of Sir Llewelyn Turner, for many a year. It was presented to him after the ship was wrecked on Caernarfon Bar on 18 October 1841, while on her way home from South America.*

she had drifted round in a circle while searching for the South Stack lighthouse.

At very low tides one can still see the remains of the 855-ton clipper *Norman Court* peeping above the sea about half a mile off Cymyran beach. Built in 1869 of composite wood and iron construction, she had raced such famous contemporaries as the *Cutty Sark*, *Thermopylae* and *Taeping* during the peak of the China trade and won the 1872 tea race with a time of ninety-six days. She was re-rigged as a barque in 1878 and was carrying a cargo of sugar from Java when she crossed Caernarfon Bay on the night of 29 March 1883. It was her first voyage under the command of Capt McBride who, at the subsequent Board of Trade inquiry, was found to be at fault in his navigation when the *Norman Court* tore out her bottom on the Crigyll rocks. Her mainmast collapsed almost immediately, smashing the ship's boats, and at daybreak the crew were seen clinging to the fore-rigging. Five attempts to fire a rocket line from the shore all fell short of the wreck. In the wind blowing that day Rhoscolyn lifeboat, less than two miles away, should have been most favourably placed to attempt a rescue but the boat was beached at Porth Diana, Trearddur Bay. She had been damaged a couple of days earlier while going to the aid of another vessel.

Rhosneigr lifeboat was nearer but would have to be rowed against the wind through the two reefs separating her from Cymyran Bay. Nevertheless she was launched and had almost reached the *Norman Court* when she was momentarily thrown on her beam ends, one man being tossed out although he saved himself by grabbing a lifeline. Exhausted and frightened, and with one of the rowlocks broken, the lifeboatmen returned to Rhosneigr. In the afternoon the Rhosneigr men were persuaded to make a second attempt but again they turned back. By this time darkness had fallen and they refused to put to sea for a third try. Answering an appeal from Col Marshall, secretary of the Rhoscolyn lifeboat, the Holyhead crew travelled by a special train to Rhosneigr where they launched the local boat and saved the clipper's twenty survivors – an effort which was rewarded with an RNLI silver medal for Coxswain Edward Jones. The particularly beautiful figurehead of the *Norman Court,* depicting a daughter of the original owners, adorned the garden of a house near Holyhead for many a year but now seems to have vanished.

A snowstorm was blamed for the loss of the 5,146 ton White Diamond steamer *Missouri* (Warren Line) on 1 March 1886. She ran ashore at Porth-y-Post, two miles east of a course which would have taken her safely past South Stack. The LSA team from Holyhead made contact with their first rocket and before long the ship's doctor, three stowaways and eighteen cattle-minders had been hauled ashore by breeches buoy. Having got rid of his 'passengers', the captain decided to keep the rest of his crew about him in the hope of saving his ship on the rising tide, but the efforts of two tugs were of no avail. As the water rose through a hole aft the ship developed a heavy list to starboard and was abandoned. Much of her wreckage is still to be found in fairly shallow water a few yards off shore.

Old warships seem to have a fatal affinity for the coast of Anglesey. HMS *Enterprise* was wrecked at Aberffraw in October 1889. She was being towed from Plymouth to Liverpool by the tug *Liverpool* and both were threatened with destruction after being swept into Caernarfon Bay before a full gale. The tug master signalled that he would have to abandon his tow and, after a prolonged and hazardous effort, the naval crew were transferred to the *Liverpool.* Soon after being cast adrift the old gunboat became a total loss. Fifty-years later HMS *Cyclops* (ex-*Indrabarah*, 1905) survived a similar incident after being cast adrift in Caernarfon Bay in a north-westerly gale. There were only eight men aboard the 11,300-ton obsolete depot ship and they were taken off by Holyhead lifeboat on 24 March 1947. Subsequently the *Cyclops* was reboarded to continue her journey to the breakers.

In 1891 a lifeboat station was established at Porth Rhuffydd, the northern tip of Caernarfon Bay. Her brief and unspectacular career began on 22 June 1894 when the crew of the SS *Mersey* refused to be rescued. The ship, homeward bound from France to Liverpool, had run aground but a short distance from the lifeboat station during heavy fog. With the nonplussed lifeboatmen still standing by, the *Mersey* slid off the rocks and sank in deep water, her crew of thirteen scrambling ashore by ladder. The lifeboat's second and last service was on 12 October of the same year, when eight of her crew were placed aboard the Norwegian barque *Eugenie* to assist in refloating the vessel.

In sharp contrast, the Rhoscolyn lifeboat was involved in many noteworthy incidents. An inscribed oar blade which, until recently, was an honoured wall decoration at a cottage in the village, commemorated the wrecking of the Lancaster schooner *J. W. Wearing* on 8 December 1901. The vessel was leaking and listing some six miles south-west of Rhoscolyn Point when the lifeboat *Ramon Cabrera* was launched. Time and again the lifeboat was manoeuvred alongside the schooner but only two men had been taken off by the time both vessels had been driven to within about 200yd of the shore. 'So I pulled the lifeboat up under her stern and the remainder of the crew (three men) jumped on board,' reported Coxswain Hugh Hughes, adding:

> I then got the sails up and only cleared Porth Saint Rocks by a boat's length. The vessel was driven on the rocks and in matchwood ten minutes after we got the three men off. Some of the crew got knocked about under the vessel's stern, we lost five oars, and got a hole in the side of the lifeboat.

The Rhosneigr lifeboat rescuing twenty men from the Norman Court in 1883.

His laconic report conceals the narrow escape of the lifeboat as it passed beneath the stern of the schooner. The two vessels were dashed together, smashing four of the oars and driving a fifth through the side of the lifeboat, trapping the lowered mast at the moment when it was essential to raise sail. Seizing an axe, George Smith severed the oar with one blow and it was this oar blade which was later preserved as a relic. A man of remarkable strength, Smith was himself rescued by the *Ramon Cabrera* on 30 August 1923, when he was over eighty years of age. Caught by a sudden gale while attending to his lobster pots, his boat was driven on to Rhoscolyn Beacon rock where it was instantly destroyed. He scrambled to safety and survived eighteen miserable hours clinging to the beacon on his sea-drenched perch.

Disaster has overtaken many North Wales lifeboats, among them the *Ramon Cabrera* which lost five men off Llanddwyn on 3 December 1920. She had been launched in response to distress signals from the Whitby steamer *Timbo*, straining at both her anchors west of Caernarfon Bar. As the anchors seemed to be holding, and several efforts to get alongside had been unsuccessful, Coxswain Owen Owens decided to make for the shelter of Llanddwyn. The men had been struggling for about an hour when a huge wave engulfed them and swept away Evan Hughes and Owen Jones. Some considerable time later the lifeboat was thrown on its beam ends and three more men vanished, William Thomas, Richard Hughes and the coxswain. The exhausted survivors had been at sea for seven hours by the time they succeeded in beaching the *Ramon Cabrera* at Llanddwyn. The five bodies all came ashore to be buried together at Rhoscolyn churchyard.

Meanwhile the *Timbo* had lost four of her crew after parting from her anchors, being buffeted across the bay and hurled high up the shingle beach at Dinas Dinlle, south of Caernarfon. After a complex salvage operation, including the laying of a launching ramp, the steamer was returned to the sea. Ironically, this tragic launch of the *Ramon Cabrera* was officially classified as a non-service and there is no mention of it on the old record board now preserved at Rhoscolyn Church House. The tiny community never really recovered from the 1920 disaster and, in February 1929, the lifeboat inspector recommended that the station should be closed 'owing to the impossibility of raising a suitable crew.'

The ship's cat was the only casualty when the Norwegian steamer *Havso* struck Maen Piscar, a rock off Rhoscolyn, on 21 July 1937. Laden with scrap iron, she sank rapidly but the crew got away in their own boat. When the steamer *Kyle Prince* ran aground at Gaethle, midway between Rhoscolyn and Llanddwyn, on 8 October 1938, she was derelict, her crew of nine having been taken off by the Holyhead lifeboat some eight miles north of Bardsey. Her troubles began when heavy seas caused flooding in the engine room and put out the furnaces. After both anchor cables had snapped, the *Kyle Prince* was at the mercy of the sea. Two years later, a similarly named ship, the *Kyle Firth*, also came to grief in Caernarfon Bay. Carrying a cargo of stone, she soon sank after running on to the rocky shore near Penrhosfeilw, but a short distance south of South Stack lighthouse - the light having been extinguished because of the war. Four of the crew got away by ship's boat and the remaining five were taken off by Holyhead lifeboat.

Navigational problems attributable to the war also caused two Canadian Lake steamers to run aground north of Llanddwyn within a few days of each other, the *Eaglescliffe Hall* on 12 November 1940, and the *Watkins F. Nisbet* on 6 December. Holyhead coastguards took off both crews by breeches buoy, thirty-three from the former and nineteen from the latter. The *Eaglescliffe Hall* was refloated four days later. The *Watkins F. Nisbet* was cut in two on the beach, where the forepart was abandoned and may still be seen. The after half, containing all the machinery, was sealed and floated during the summer of 1941 to be towed through the Menai Strait first to Port Dinorwig and later on to Birkenhead.

Radar and modern engines have eliminated most of the problems of navigating the Irish Sea but the western coast of Anglesey can still produce a few surprises. The 7,279-ton *Bobara* ran on to the rocks in Cymyran Bay in calm weather on 24 January 1955. Thirty-three of the crew were taken off by breeches buoy, the captain and three officers remaining on board until she was refloated three days later. Royal Air Force rescue launch *1659* put up distress flares five miles south-west of South Stack on 26 January 1970. Her engines had failed after a long mercy dash into the Irish Sea to pick up the civilian crew of a balloon. Holyhead lifeboat took the launch in tow after she had been located by a helicopter of 22 Search and Rescue Squadron from RAF Station Valley – the modern name for the former dreaded territory of the Crigyll outlaws.

To the confusion of future historians, Llanddwyn's navigation light was transferred in 1972 from the 1846 lighthouse (with its lantern in a ground-level lean-to extension), to the top of the 23ft high beacon tower of 1819. Thus the older beacon became a lighthouse, while the lighthouse reverted to an unlit beacon – the purpose for which it was built in 1845.

In November 1974 the Prince of Wales completed his helicopter pilot's training at RAF Valley by removing the historic Llanddwyn signalling gun, for his test in lifting and carrying an underslung load. The gun was taken to Valley, where it seemed destined to stay as an officers' mess trophy. The writer (once an RAF officer) protested, in the columns of the *Daily Post*, that the gun was a memorial to the lifeboatmen and pilots of Llanddwyn, for which purpose it was left in situ after the RNLI presented it to the last station secretary in 1907. Somewhat belatedly a school was persuaded to make a new wooden carriage for the gun, which was returned to Llanddwyn in 1976, although to a bogus new location outside the old cottages.

Anglesey's western shore can still produce a few surprises like the stranding on Holyhead Island in 1955 of the 7,279-ton Bobara (ex-Sedgepool, ex-Samdart) of London.

HOLYHEAD creek enjoyed a few decades of ancient naval glory as the fortified western extremity of the Roman Empire and then slipped into a millennium of obscurity until 1579. In that year Queen Elizabeth I, great-great-grand-daughter of Owen Tudor, of Penmynydd, awarded £10 per lunar month to Richard White, her post-horse master at Beaumaris, for him to maintain a barque at Holyhead to convey packets of State papers to Dublin as and when required.

The Holyhead-Dublin ferry has been maintained ever since, with occasional interruptions due to war, politics, commercial intrigue or an extraordinary run of disaster and shipping losses. Our earliest record of misfortune involving a Holyhead post barque is for 1618 when Capt Robert Pepper, who had held the contract for at least ten years, was allowed £13 6s 8d (£13.33) compensation for serious damage to his vessel. Capt Langford took over the packet contract in 1628 and three years later suffered the indignity of having his vessel robbed by Arab pirates.

Irish Royalists captured the post barque *Patrick* in 1649 but by that time the king was dead and Holyhead was in the iron grip of Major Thomas Swift. As military governor, church-warden and Parliamentary Commissioner for the Propagation of the Gospel, he installed the garrison in the parish church which lay within the walls of the original Roman fort. In 1650 he became postmaster, acquired the ownership of the packet boats and built a fine new inn to house and feed travellers arriving at his creek – the house surviving until April 1941 when it was destroyed by a German bomb. In 1652 we find Major Swift complaining that the Admiralty had seized the wreck of one of his post barques after it had been cast ashore. Pirates operating within full view of the garrison captured two of his barques in 1656 and seized everything removable, including clothing, before sending the two masters into Holyhead to obtain £50 with which to buy back their vessels. Major Swift paid up, knowing that the alternative would be to watch his barques burning before the town. Seemingly marauders were still troubling him in 1658 for in that year he extended the church belfry by 17ft to give the garrison a watch tower.

Like the Romans before him, Major Swift vanished into obscurity with the restoration of the monarchy in 1660, although a man named John Swift obtained the first Holyhead-Dublin packet contract under Charles II at a fee of £400 a year. It was he who lost a post barque together with 120 passengers in 1670, evidence of the extent of the ferry traffic. In August 1680 the first customs officer was appointed to Holyhead at a salary of £10 a year to control what was described as 'great quantities of Irish cattle' being imported there in contravention of an Act prohibiting any such import into Britain.

The *Grace*, one of the three packet boats maintained at Holyhead under the 1689 contract of James Vickers, was captured by the French privateers *Swift* and *St Martin* while anchored in Dublin Bay on 25 July 1692. She was completely stripped before her hull was sold back to Vickers for fifty guineas (£52.50). Two Holyhead packet boats, the *Ann* and the *Pembroke*, disappeared without trace while making the crossing in September 1710.

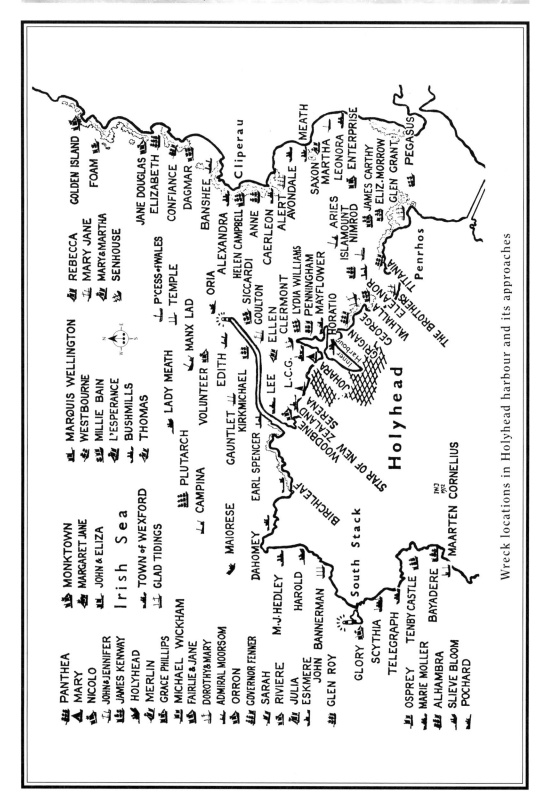

Wreck locations in Holyhead harbour and its approaches

A touch of comedy surrounded the activities of a French privateer off Holyhead on 6 October 1710. She arrived flying English colours and firing guns which Maurice Owen, the customs officer, took to be distress signals. On going out to the stranger Owen and his colleagues were made prisoner and their boat was hoisted aboard the Frenchman, which then sailed away. One assumes that after questioning the prisoners as to the town's defences and cash resources the privateer would have returned to offer Holyhead the choice between bombardment or paying ransom. However things worked out rather differently, for the privateer was driven back on the following day, dismasted and out of control, to be wrecked on the rock-strewn shore of Penrhos Point a mile east of the harbour. At least fourteen guns were heaved overboard to reduce her list and others were fired intermittently throughout the night while people on shore argued as to whether the noise was intended to be a warning or an appeal for help. As the storm abated at daybreak seven Holyhead boats went out to the wreck and took off 150 men, including Maurice Owen and his colleagues. The seamen were marched to Beaumaris gaol – never designed for such an influx – while the officers were placed on board the surviving packet boat *James* and sent to Dublin as prisoners.

Holyhead was given a boost in 1772 when the Post Office ended monopoly contracts and increased the number of packet boats to six by awarding warrants to the masters of 'good and sufficient' vessels. Two such vessels, the *Bessborough* and *Hillsborough,* were captured by the American privateer *Black Prince* on 8 March 1780 and cost the Post Office a total of £1,067 in ransom and compensation for stolen equipment. The 1772 reorganisation, which also involved road improvements on the route to Holyhead, did not deter Holyhead's traditional rivals for the Irish traffic at Parkgate, on the Cheshire shore of the Dee estuary. On 18 December 1790 the 70-ton *Clermont,* of Parkgate, was wrecked on Salt Island, at the mouth of Holyhead harbour, with the loss of 110 lives.

A Dutch galliot, *Die Liebe,* was wrecked on Penrhos beach in January 1802 followed, in the February, by a Liverpool vessel *The Brothers,* but the storms of that winter were seemingly as nothing compared with a gale in 1807 described from Penrhos mansion by Lady Maria Josepha Stanley. In a letter to a relative she said it was the worst storm she had witnessed in twenty-five years. She watched a three-masted ship and two brigs miss the harbour entrance and strike the rocks opposite her home where they were soon dashed to pieces. Lady Maria also recorded the remarkable escape of a remarkable man, American-born Capt John Macgregor Skinner, who dominated the Holyhead maritime scene for thirty-three years and whose memorial obelisk now overlooks the modern harbour.

Skinner was born in 1760 at Perth Amboy, New Jersey, where his father was the provincial attorney-general. He was commissioned into the Royal Navy aboard HMS *Phoenix* in 1776 and lost an arm soon afterwards, fighting his fellow-colonists in the American War of Independence. Later he lost an eye in battle, but despite his Nelsonian disabilities he arrived at Holyhead in 1799 to take command of one of the Post Office packets. 'He can shuffle the cards better with his remaining left hand than I can with both of mine,' noted another of the Penrhos family.

In the great gale of 1807 Capt Skinner combined all his skill, local knowledge and daring to fight his way into Holyhead harbour through the rock-strewn sound which then separated Salt Island from the mouth of the creek, a feat which earned the congratulations of all who had witnessed it.

With the Act of Union of the Parliaments of Great Britain and Ireland in 1801 Holyhead assumed an even more important role, and a constant flow of influential passengers led to a series of improvements at the port. South Stack was equipped with a red light which shone for the first time on 9 February 1809, more as a beckoning beacon than as a warning. In 1810 Sir John Rennie began the conversion of the natural creek into a harbour available at all states of the tide. He did this by closing the gap through which Capt Skinner had escaped in

1807 and building the Admiralty Pier, extending some 1,000ft from Salt Island (now the car ferry terminal). Coincidental with the completion of the pier, the Post Office introduced two paddle-steamers, the *Lightning* and the *Meteor* in June 1821.

In the following August the new service received an unexpected royal inauguration. It had been made known that King George IV would put into Holyhead, to visit the Marquess of Anglesey, while on his way to Ireland aboard the *Royal George*. On 7 August he stepped ashore to a royal salute fired with ninepounder guns salvaged from the French privateer wrecked in 1710. (Another of the guns was raised in December 1967 by members of the Merseyside branch of the British Sub-Aqua Club.) After being stranded for five days by unfavourable winds, the King discovered that the two steam packets were unaffected by the weather. Abandoning his becalmed navy, the King took passage aboard the *Lightning* and was so delighted with his first steamer trip that he renamed the humble 8-knot paddler the *Royal Sovereign King George IV* (later shortened, for convenience, to *Royal Sovereign*). Her master, the redoubtable Capt Skinner, was offered a knighthood for his services but upon explaining that lack of financial means prevented his supporting such a title he was awarded the more lucrative rank of Captain, Royal Navy (Retired), with appropriate pension. Capt Skinner was seventy-two years of age when he was swept overboard and drowned while bringing the PS *Escape* into Holyhead on 13 October 1832. Five years later the ship which George IV had

The SS **Marie Moller**, *of Shanghai, caught fire in Caernarfon Bay on 22 March 1927. She managed to steam as far as Holy Island where her crew of 82 was taken off, leaving her to drift ashore, blazing from stem to stern.*

honoured with his own name was transferred to the Admiralty and given the somewhat strange name of *Monkey*.

Another major development at Holyhead was the introduction of the semaphore telegraph, described in Chapter One, to keep the Liverpool merchants informed of impending arrivals. A ship belonging to the famous New York firm of Fish, Grinnell & Co was the first to be reported in this way. According to an advertisement in the New York *Journal of Commerce*, the *Napoleon* was due to sail from her South Street pier on 8 October 1827. Her arrival off Holyhead was noted on 26 October and the news was relayed to Liverpool within fifteen minutes.

It was at about this time that the Nimrod rocks, 300yd off shore opposite Penrhos beach, derived their name from the wreck of HMS *Nimrod*, an 18-gun sloop of the 'Cruizer' class. There were no casualties and at the subsequent court martial the commanding officer was absolved of blame, the accident being attributed to the breaking of an anchor. The wreck was sold to the salvage firm of Rowland, Robert & Co.

The notable record of service of Holyhead lifeboat station began on 28 April 1829 when, in conjunction with shore-based life-saving apparatus, twenty-three people were saved from the vessels *Harlequin* and *Fame*. The RNLI gold medal was awarded to Capt William Owen, of the local brig *Stanley*, who took charge of the lifeboat for the rescue, on 10 September 1835, of eleven men from the ship *Plutarch*, of New Orleans, wrecked west of the town.

Many serious collisions have occurred off Holyhead. The first for which we have a record was in February 1841 when the barque *Governor Fenner*, carrying intending emigrants for America, was lost with 122 lives after being struck by the SS *Nottingham*.

As an integral part of Parliament's plan for London and Dublin to be connected by the fastest and most certain form of transport, the Chester & Holyhead Railway (soon to be bought by the London & North Western Railway Co) arrived at Holyhead in 1848, along with four new paddle steamers, the *Hibernia*, *Scotia*, *Anglia* and *Cambria*. However, the lowest tender for the carriage of the mail across the Irish Sea was that of the City of Dublin Steam Packet Co, so that Holyhead became a busy little harbour as the rivals vied for the uncommitted passenger traffic.

The SS *Town of Wexford* was seen to be flying distress signals shortly before she struck the rocky shore west of Holyhead on 4 January 1852. Unable to row out of the harbour against the gale, the lifeboat was towed to the scene by the *Anglia* and, in the course of several trips, saved forty-three lives. A Belfast barque, the *Penningham*, bound from Liverpool to Rio de Janeiro with a cargo of coal, was wrecked on Salt Island as she endeavoured to make for the harbour entrance on 18 February 1854. Her crew of eleven were rescued. The 1,700-ton wooden ship *John Bannerman*, laden with cotton for Liverpool, was wrecked between the North and South Stacks on 3 March 1855. The mate and six men who left the wreck in the ship's boat were never seen again but much of the cargo came ashore as loose cotton, which was described as having the appearance of snow two to three feet deep.

Today Holyhead has the added protection of the 1.8 mile long breakwater which encloses the New Harbour. Construction began in 1845 and was to last for twenty-eight years, but by May of 1857 enough had been done for the commander designate and owners of the enormous SS *Great Eastern* (which had then been on the stocks for three years) to visit Anglesey 'with view of judging as to the eligibility of the new harbour for the departure of this leviathan ship on her first voyage across the Atlantic.' *(Illustrated London News, 6 June 1857.)* Two years later this 18,915-ton monster – the largest ship until the launching of the White Star liner *Celtic* in 1901 – was battling for survival at Holyhead.

At the end of her unpropitious sea trials the *Great Eastern* was anchored close to the unfinished Holyhead breakwater on 10 October 1859 for the inspection of all who wished to see her. Visitors included Prince Albert, consort of Queen Victoria, who came by train on the seventeenth, and the Emperor Louis Napoleon of France, who arrived aboard his war steamer *Dauphin* on the following day. The *Great Eastern* was still at anchor on 25 October for the *Royal Charter* gale. Capt William Harrison, her 47-year-old Cumberland-born commander, remained on the bridge of his ship throughout the night, and though he kept her steaming into wind to ease the strain on the anchors, one of the cables parted nevertheless, causing considerable anxiety. One by one the saloon skylights were shattered and as the sea came pouring in with each wave a *Times* reporter, who happened to be on board, recorded the scene. Masts protruding from the sea told him that at least one large vessel had sunk at anchor. Another four had been swept into a shallow corner of the harbour where they were rolling violently, soon to disintegrate. He watched the heavy scaffolding, railway and cranes at the unfinished end of the breakwater topple into the sea, adding to the mass of debris which had already forced Capt Harrison to stop his paddles for fear of piercing the side of his own ship. However the *Great Eastern* rode out the storm on her screw and one anchor and sailed on 2 November for Southampton – where Capt Harrison was drowned two months later.

A collision at Holyhead in October 1861 nearly exposed the secret activities of James Bulloch, a former United States Navy officer who had arrived at Liverpool four months earlier to buy ships and munitions for the Confederate cause in the American Civil War. By the time he booked in at a seafront hotel at Holyhead he had already bought and despatched several ships and had placed an order with Laird, of Birkenhead for the building of the notorious *Alabama*. He had gone to Holyhead to evade the Union spies who were temporarily concentrating their attention on the Clyde where Bulloch had bought the 460-ton schooner-rigged steamer *Fingal*. On 11 October the *Fingal* sailed under the British flag, with customs clearance for the Bahamas. Her only passenger was Scottish-born John Low, of Savannah, who was serving as a private in the Georgia Hussars when posted to Liverpool in July 1861 for special service under Bulloch. In the Irish Sea, Low, who had obtained his master's ticket five years earlier, took command as agent for the new owners. The *Fingal* had on board 15,000 rifles, 500 revolvers, 3,000 sabres, two 4.5in guns, two 2.5in guns and millions of rounds of ammunition. She was heavily laden when she rounded Holyhead breakwater soon after midnight on the 14th and rammed an anchored Austrian brig, the *Siccardi*, which sank with all hands in the New Harbour.

Realising the probable consequences of staying around for a daytime investigation into the collision, Low himself went ashore to rouse Bulloch from his bed. In the dead of night Bulloch, together with a Confederate colonel and a Texan doctor going home to join the army, settled their hotel bill and boarded the *Fingal*. 'I thought of the rifles and sabres in the hold and the ill-armed pickets on the Potomac, waiting and longing for them and told the captain to weigh anchor at once,' wrote Bulloch. It was daybreak as the *Fingal* steamed out of Holyhead to become the Confederate ironclad *Atlanta*.

During the course of several similar cloak and dagger missions Bulloch and Low arranged for the disappearance from Holyhead of the 470-ton London & North Western Railway paddle steamers *Anglia* and *Scotia* which had been surplus to the Irish ferry requirements ever since their delivery thirteen years earlier. Both crossed the Atlantic in 1861. They were captured by the Union navy in October 1862 to become the *Admiral Du Pont* and *General Banks*, respectively. Reverting to Confederate ownership, the ex-*Anglia* was re-named *Fanny & Jane* and eventually was sunk while engaged in blockade-running.

This was the start of a long run of misfortune for the London & North Western Railway Co. Trapped by fog, their paddle steamer *Telegraph* ran aground near South Stack on 17 April 1863. Fifty passengers and several of the crew of twenty-seven were taken off by small boats which put out from the shore, but the ship was later refloated and put back into service. Two LNWR paddlers, the *Edith* and the *Duchess of Sutherland*, collided off the end of

Holyhead breakwater on 8 September 1875. The *Edith*, 875 tons, sank rapidly in the New Harbour with the loss of two of her crew and, for the next two years, resisted several attempts to raise her. She was eventually lifted to the surface on 8 December 1877 and returned to service in the following December, being converted into a turbine twin-screw ship in 1885 and going to the breakers in 1912 – four years after the *Duchess of Sutherland*. Another LNWR paddle steamer, the *Earl Spencer*, 909 tons, collided with and sank the iron-built Llanelly schooner *Merlin* near the breakwater on 17 October 1875.

The *Aries*, a 145-ton steam yacht owned by Sir James Ramsden, managing director of the Barrow Iron Shipbuilding Co, sank off Holyhead in 1880. Named by Lady Ramsden, she was the first vessel to be launched from the yards that were to become famous for their warships. Raised and modified, the *Aries* returned to Barrow docks as a tug (not to be confused with a new luxury yacht of the same name ordered by Sir James in 1880).

Collisions remained the big hazard for the Holyhead ferry boats and both the SS *Holyhead* and the German barque *Alhambra* were lost in this way on 31 October 1883. The *Holyhead*, an 842-ton screw steamer belonging to the LNWR, was returning from Dublin with a cargo of 300 pigs and 17 horses. The *Alhambra*, of Pillau, was sailing from Liverpool for New York, with a ballast of 700 tons of coal, when the mate mistook the masthead light of the steamer for a distant land light and turned the barque across the bows of the *Holyhead*. Capt C. W. Hicks put his engines to full astern but still ploughed through the German, one of whose crew scrambled aboard the *Holyhead* before the vessels parted. The *Alhambra* sank quickly with the loss of eighteen lives, including her master, Capt Dietritz, and his 17-year-old daughter. Six men were rescued from the water by the *Holyhead* but it soon became obvious that she, too, must sink. She was abandoned, with a quartermaster and young deckhand still trapped in the forecastle, and sank within twenty minutes of the collision. The survivors were picked up by the Caernarfon schooner *Gertrude* fifteen miles off South Stack and taken into Holyhead.

Smarting under their second failure to secure the mail contract between Holyhead and Dublin, with consequent wasteful competition for passenger traffic, the LNWR decided to develop their trump card – their railway monopoly. Between 1875 and 1880 they built a new passenger terminal and deepened the old Holyhead creek to create what is now known as the Inner Harbour, with quay walls which are also railway platforms, sharing the same canopy roof. Thus passengers who chose to use the LNWR steamers need walk only a few sheltered paces from their railway carriage. The advantage was temporarily lost to the railway during the stormy and incident-filled night of 1 February 1884. Holed on some rocks off Salt Island, in the New Harbour, the SS *Horatio*, bound from Barrow to Calais, was taken in tow with the intention of beaching her between the Old Harbour and Inner Harbour. She foundered across the mouth of the latter, trapping one LNWR steamer within and preventing another from entering. In the same gale the schooner *Woodbine*, sheltering in the New Harbour while bound from Charlestown to Fleetwood, parted from her cable and was driven ashore. Meanwhile the heavily-laden barque *Grigan*, bound for Pernambuco, was wrecked on Peibio rocks opposite the head of Admiralty Pier.

Capt Britt, of the Littlehampton brig *Robert & Mary*, took four of his crew in a small boat with the intention of offering assistance to the *Grigan*, but as they pulled away from the dry dock they were run down by the LNWR cattle steamer *Alexandra*. The captain died under one of the paddle wheels but the other men survived.

By comparison with the LNWR the ships of the rival City of Dublin Steam Packet Co seemed to enjoy a charmed existence. There was some concern when their *Leinster*, bearing the prestige prefix 'Royal Mail Ship,' was one hour and fifteen minutes late arriving at Holyhead during these February storms, but the LNWR steamer *Shamrock*, making the same passage, was exactly twice as late. On 1 May 1884 the *Leinster* was some eight miles out of Holyhead when her port engine shaft broke, but even then the tug *Knight of the Cross*

One of the many wooden wrecks that littered the coast around Holyhead by the end of the 19th century, nearly all losing their identity during the course of time.

The schooner Grace Phillips was one of 57 vessels built on the beach at Porthdinllaen. She was sailing in ballast when wrecked on Cliperau Rocks, near Holyhead, on 25 February 1898.

happened to be steaming by to tow her back to Holyhead. The LNWR lost another steamer, the 800-ton *Admiral Moorsom,* which sank rapidly with the loss of five lives after a collision with the American ship *Santa Clara* off Holyhead on 15 January 1885.

Lifeboat Saturday, the annual fund-raising effort in aid of the RNLI, had its origins in the tragic events of 9 December 1886. Of the many lifeboat volunteers who put to sea that night twenty-six men of the St Anne's and Southport crews were drowned. The gale was no less violent at Holyhead where three vessels were wrecked: the SS *Avondale* on Penrhyn Point, the Norwegian barque *Dagmar* in Porth Tywyn Mawr, and the Liverpool ship *Pegasus* on Traeth y Gribin, where Coxswain Edward Jones, of Holyhead lifeboat, won the RNLI silver medal for rescuing the crew of twenty-one.

Continuing their extraordinary maritime adventures, the LNWR managed to put two paddle-steamers aground outside Holyhead on 4 January 1887: the *Banshee,* of 1,221 tons, which ran ashore in Porth Tywyn while returning from Ireland with 266 passengers and a crew of 44, and the *Eleanor,* 854 tons, which endeavoured to tow her off in dense fog. Both were subsequently refloated. As though in celebration of the anniversary of this epic, the LNWR steamer *Earl Spencer* ran onto the rocks forming the apron for the outside of the Holyhead breakwater on 8 January 1888. In answer to the ship's distress rocket, fired in dense fog, coastguard Chief Officer Williams ran almost the full length of the breakwater to find her firmly wedged, bows on, some 12yd out to sea. A breeches buoy was quickly set up, without the need for a rocket, and thirty-four passengers were landed, including a shipwrecked crew picked up earlier in the day in the Irish Sea. Another seven passengers were taken off by lifeboat and later the steamer was hauled clear with a big hole in her bows.

The name of John O. Williams, whom we also met in the last chapter, is still revered at Holyhead. Born at Bosherston, Pembrokeshire, in 1844, he joined the Royal Navy when he was fifteen and served at sea until 1870. He was then drafted to the coastguard service which, at that time, was the first naval reserve. He served at Rhosneigr during 1876-8 and returned to Anglesey in 1884 to serve as chief officer at Holyhead until 1890. Fearless on a cliff face or in a small boat, and an acknowledged expert in the use of rocket apparatus, he received twelve lifesaving awards including the RNLI silver medal and bar, Board of Trade silver medal, Liverpool Mercantile Marine Association medal, Liverpool Shipwreck & Humane Society medal and the cross of the Ordre du Devoir.

In those days wrecks were almost predictable and when northerly winds developed into a gale on 10 February 1889 John Williams distributed his men in anticipation of trouble. Shortly after midnight the lookout on Mael jetty reported that a schooner had parted from her cable. Williams fired the maroon to launch the lifeboat and four men were taken off before the vessel struck the southern shore of the bay. She was the *Enterprise,* of Dublin. Within the hour the barque *Glen Grant,* of Halifax, NS, also parted from her cable while anchored in the New Harbour with a cargo from Pensacola. She was soon among the rocks of Penrhos, 190yd from where Williams was already waiting with his LSA team. The first rocket struck the figurehead, two fell short, but the fourth found the rigging to enable the crew of thirteen to be hauled ashore where each man was greeted with a tot of brandy from Lord Stanley's butler. The last of Williams' many rescues at Holyhead was on the night of 17 December 1889 when, after climbing down a 150ft cliff at Penrhosfeilw, south of South Stack, he and four of his men each earned the RNLI silver medal by putting to sea in a small boat to pick up three survivors from the Liverpool barque *Tenby Castle* which had broken up about 500yd off shore.

Williams' last achievement, before leaving Wales to become divisional officer at Aldeburgh, in Suffolk was to persuade the RNLI that one lifeboat was insufficient at Holyhead. A second station was opened there in 1890 followed, in 1892, by yet a third station equipped with the Institution's first steam lifeboat, the *Duke of Northumberland.*

Coxswain Robert Jones of the original, or No 1, lifeboat station was fatally injured in a sequel to the wrecking of the Sunderland steamer *Meath* on Penrhyn Point on 1 February 1892. Overloaded after rescuing the crew of thirty-eight, the lifeboat *Thomas Fielden* could make no progress and Coxswain Jones decided to beach her, a manoeuvre which was accomplished without mishap. It was on the following day, during an attempt to refloat her, that the *Thomas Fielden* was hurled back to the beach, crushing the coxswain.

This corner of the island was to keep the lifeboats busy in succeeding years. The Cunard liner *Scythia*, with forty passengers on board, ran aground south of South Stack on New Year's Day, 1896. She managed to get off under her own power but the Harrison liner *Editor* became a total loss soon after striking the same shore on 22 March 1897 while inward bound with a cargo of cotton and sugar. On 28 November of the same year the barque *Alert*, of St John, New Bunswick, outward bound from Preston, was wrecked on Penrhyn Point.

Sixty tons of explosives were removed from the African Steamship Co's *Dahomey* after she caught fire while aground between the breakwater and North Stack in April 1898. She ran aground in thick fog on the 6th, her nine passengers and crew of thirty being taken off by the *Duke of Northumberland*, which also made two trips to salvage mail.

The LNWR paddle steamer *Eleanor* was in trouble again on 23 June 1900. Returning from Dublin with 750 Irish harvesters she rammed the 1,106-ton *Connemara*, also belonging to the LNWR, just off the end of Holyhead breakwater as the latter set out for Greenore with 129 passengers. Both ships remained locked together for a few minutes, the crumpled bows of the paddler wedged into the port side of the *Connemara* abaft the bridge. Miraculously there were no injuries and the two vessels were able to return to Holyhead for repairs. The ill-fated *Connemara* rammed and sank the Liverpool cargo steamer *Marquis of Bute* off the Skerries on 20 March 1910, and was herself sunk with the loss of all fifty-one passengers and thirty-one crew when struck by the *Retriever*, a small collier, soon after leaving Greenore for Holyhead on 3 November 1916.

Lighthouse keepers at South Stack have witnessed many tragedies but none more poignant than the loss of the 2,520-ton Liverpool barque *Primrose Hill* on 28 December 1900. Capt J. Wilson had with him a crew of thirty-three, including twelve apprentices, when he left the Mersey for Australia on Christmas Eve, using the tug *William Jolliffe* to tow him to the open sea. At dawn on the 28th the tug put into Holyhead to say she had lost her tow off Bardsey during the night. At 8.30 am a telegraphist at South Stack spotted the barque, caught between a gale and an opposing flood tide, and flying the distress flags 'NC' as she drifted ever nearer the cliffs. The LNWR steamer *Hibernia*, near the end of her crossing from Dublin, drew alongside and rescue seemed certain until the steamer's steering gear chose that moment to break down. It was as much as the master could do to extricate his own passenger laden ship – without those on the barque or on land knowing the reason for his withdrawal. Dragging her anchors within 200yd of South Stack, and with her crew waving to those on shore, the *Primrose Hill* eventually struck a submerged rock at the opposite end of the bay at about 2.00 pm and broke up in five minutes with the loss of all but one of her crew.

With the outbreak of war in 1914 the Admiralty requisitioned all four LNWR passenger steamers at Holyhead and had them converted locally into armed boarding cruisers, each equipped with three 6-pounder guns. The *Hibernia* became HMS *Tara*, and was torpedoed by the *U-35* in the Mediterranean on 5 November 1915. HMS *Anglia* was paid off in April 1915, disarmed and converted into a hospital ship, in which capacity she struck a mine in the Straits of Dover on 18 November 1915, sinking with the loss of eighty lives. The *Snowdon*, a cargo ship which remained with the LNWR, was struck amidships by a torpedo which failed to explode while crossing from Holyhead to Dublin.

The railway-owned *Slieve Bawn* went to the aid of the 21,000-ton White Star liner *Celtic* when she was torpedoed or mined south of the Isle of Man on 15 February 1917. Passengers

The 2,520-ton barque **Primrose Hill**, *seen here in dock at Liverpool, had twelve apprentices among her crew of thirty-three when wrecked within sight of South Stack lighthouse in 1900. There was only one survivor.*

Seven of the crew were drowned when the barque **Kirkmichael** struck Holyhead breakwater on 23 December 1893

were landed at Holyhead while the crippled liner was towed to Liverpool. In the following year the *Slieve Bawn* was attacked by gunfire from a surfaced submarine but managed to escape. The tanker *Birchleaf* was torpedoed near the Skerries on 23 February 1918 and set on fire. After her crew of twenty-nine had been taken off she was towed by two naval drifters and beached north-east of the town. The *Florrieston*, owned by W. S. Miller & Co, of Glasgow, was torpedoed and sunk six miles off South Stack on 20 April 1918. A torpedo narrowly missed the *Rosstrevor* when thirteen miles west of Holyhead on 3 May 1918.

The LNWR steamer *Slieve Bloom* was run down by the USS *Stockton* four miles west of South Stack at midnight on 20 March 1918. Her cargo of 370 cattle and 12 horses was lost with the ship, but all passengers and crew were rescued by the American ship. The *Stockton*, a destroyer engaged on antisubmarine patrol in the Irish Sea, had to proceed to HM Dockyard, Portsmouth, for substantial bow repairs, a fact which was recalled twenty-two years later when she became HMS *Ludlow*. Describing the transfer to Philip Goodhart, author of *Fifty Ships that Saved the World* (1965), Vice-Admiral Sir Guy Sayer said he was greeted by the *Stockton's* commanding officer, Lt-Cdr Lewis R. Miller, USN, with: 'Say, Cap'n, d'you know your ship has got a British bow?' She was the oldest of the American destroyers handed over to the Royal Navy at Halifax, NS, in October 1940. She survived the war and went to the breakers in 1945.

The greatest disaster involving the Holyhead ships was the torpedoing of the City of Dublin Steam Packet Co's *Leinster* with the loss of 501 lives, midway between Dublin and Holyhead, on 10 October 1918. The luck of the company had changed and in 1920 they lost the coveted mail contract and vanished from the Welsh scene.

The Post Office contract had expired in 1915 but because of the war was renewed annually until 1920, in which year the LNWR undercut their old rival by some 30 per cent. On 28 November the new 3,467-ton twin-screw *Anglia* became a 'Royal Mail Ship,' an honour for which her original predecessor of the same name had been designed seventy-three years earlier. She carried the LNWR jinx and, on 15 January 1922, was seriously damaged when she struck the Holyhead breakwater. She was withdrawn in 1924 and went to the breakers in 1935, having done no more than two years total effective work. Her sister ship *Hibernia*, also of 1920 vintage, was threatened with destruction during a severe gale on 14 January 1923, the month in which her ownership was transferred to the new amalgamation known as the London Midland & Scottish Railway Co. She broke away from her moorings and was being driven towards the breakwater when the cargo ship *Rosstrevor*, which happened to have steam up, gave chase and got a line aboard.

A Norwegian steamer, the *Asmund*, inward bound for Manchester with a cargo of grain, was holed on a rock at Porth-y-post on the south-western shore of Holy Island on 2 December 1930. Abandoned by her crew, she was later reboarded and towed to Holyhead only to sink in the New Harbour. She was raised and beached at Porth Penrhyn Mawr where her remains may still be seen. A spectacular wreck of the inter-war years was the SS *Marie Moller*, of Shanghai, which caught fire in Caernarfon Bay on 22 March 1937. She got as far as the north-western corner of Holy Island where, after the rescue of her crew of eighty-two, she drifted ashore blazing from stem to stern.

HMS *Campina*, a 290-ton naval auxiliary patrol trawler stationed at Holyhead, struck a mine a few yards from the New Harbour lighthouse and sank on 22 July 1940. The 1,598-ton SS *Meath* (ex-*Lady Meath*), carrying cattle and sheep, was mined close to the end of the breakwater on 16 August 1940 and sank a mile north-east of the lighthouse where a buoy now marks the wreck. HMS *Manx Lad*, a patrol boat sent to her aid, struck another mine and also sank at the entrance to the New Harbour. Using her own guns, the railway steamer *Cambria* beat off a German bomber on 19 December 1940, but not before one of her officers had been killed by machine-gun fire. In the following year she was attacked by a submarine

John Bannerman was a full-rigged ship of 1,700 tons, registered at St.John. She was carrying a cargo of cotton for Liverpool when she ran aground between the North and South Stacks, Holyhead, on 3 March 1855. The mate and six men who left the wreck in a boat were never seen again. When the storm abated the beach was up to three feet deep in loose cotton.

soon after leaving Holyhead with a full load of passengers but by skilful handling Capt A. Marsh evaded the enemy and the ship survived the war.

German submarines remained active in this zone until the very end of the war. An inward-bound transatlantic convoy of 17 ships was attacked by the *U-1024,* while rounding the north-western tip of Anglesey, off Holyhead, late in the afternoon of 7 April 1945. The United States-registered SS *James W. Nesmith* was badly holed by a torpedo, flooding the engine room, and bringing her to a standstill. During the night she was successfully lashed to the side of a Canadian corvette and pushed through stormy seas into Holyhead. She was the last victim of the *U-1024* for by that stage in the 1939-45 war the advantage was usually with the hunters, once they were alerted to the presence of a submarine.

The chain-damaged bows of the MV Nafsiporos are visible as a she waits in the lock to enter Langton Dock, Liverpool, after her rescue off Anglesey by the tug Utrecht, in 1966. (see page 84).

NORTHERN ANGLESEY

6

ANGLESEY'S northern shore presents the mariner with a baffling combination of havens and hazards. The former, all with good shelter from the prevailing westerly winds, include Cemlyn Bay, Cemaes Bay, Bull Bay, Amlwch Port and Moelfre Road. The hazards range from cruel cliffs such as Carmel Head or Point Lynas to rocky outcrops like the Skerries, Harry's Furlong, Coal Rock or the treacherous trio West Mouse, Middle Mouse and East Mouse.

The Skerries or Ynysoedd y Moelrhoniaid to give them their correct Welsh name, meaning Seal Islands – lie nearly two miles off the north-western corner of Anglesey. They form a tight cluster half a mile long and a quarter of a mile wide in the middle of the busy route into Liverpool. Viscount Thurles, father of the first Duke of Ormonde, was drowned in a shipwreck here on 15 December 1619. By a strange coincidence Sir Richard Preston, Earl of Desmond, father of the first Duchess of Ormonde, was also drowned on the Skerries on 28 October 1628 while sailing to Liverpool.

The Earl of Meath was among the thirty-five casualties when Britain's first Royal Yacht, the *Mary*, was wrecked on the Skerries while on passage from Dublin to the Dee in March 1675. Much has been written about her pioneer racing exploits in the Thames but the wreck of the *Mary* lay forgotten until accidentally discovered in 40ft of water during July 1971. The 'jaght' was a Dutch design and when Charles II sailed from Breda in such a vessel, to join the English fleet for his 1660 restoration to the throne of his beheaded father, he commented that he would not rest until he had a jaght of his own. Mr van Vlooswyck, mayor of Amsterdam, took the hint and bought the 100-ton burthen *Mary* from the Dutch East India Co. The *Mary* and a smaller jaght, the *Bezan,* were presented to the king for his pleasure and thus was yacht racing introduced to Britain, as noted in the diaries of Samuel Pepys, Secretary of the Navy.

By the time she was wrecked on the Skerries the *Mary* had been sold to the Royal Navy. She was still carrying two of her original very ornate bronze guns 5ft 11in long, and with a 3.5in bore, cast in Amsterdam in 1660. Weighing 600 lb each, these guns were found in 1971, together with an anchor, some 100yd north-east of the wreck, telling their own story of the struggle three centuries earlier to hold the *Mary* off the dreaded rocks. From the actual wreck rival groups of divers recovered seven identical bronze guns 5ft 6in long, and with a 3in bore, cast in the Tower of London with the cypher of Sir William Compton, Master of the Royal Ordnance from 1660 to 1663.

Once the property of the See of Bangor, the Skerries were diverted by Bishop Nicholas Robinson (l566-85) into the ownership of his son. In 1713 William Robinson, of Mynachdy, on Carmel Head, a descendant of the Bishop, gave a ninety-nine years lease of the islands to William Trench, who was born in Ireland in 1642. With letters patent from Queen Anne, authorising him to charge a penny per ton upon all vessels other than warships benefitting from his venture, Trench built a coal beacon on the islands and displayed his first light on 4 November 1716. Dues which Trench managed to collect were insufficient even to meet maintenance costs and he died penniless in 1725 – also heirless for his son was drowned while ferrying coal to the islands. The beacon passed to distant relatives who obtained an Act

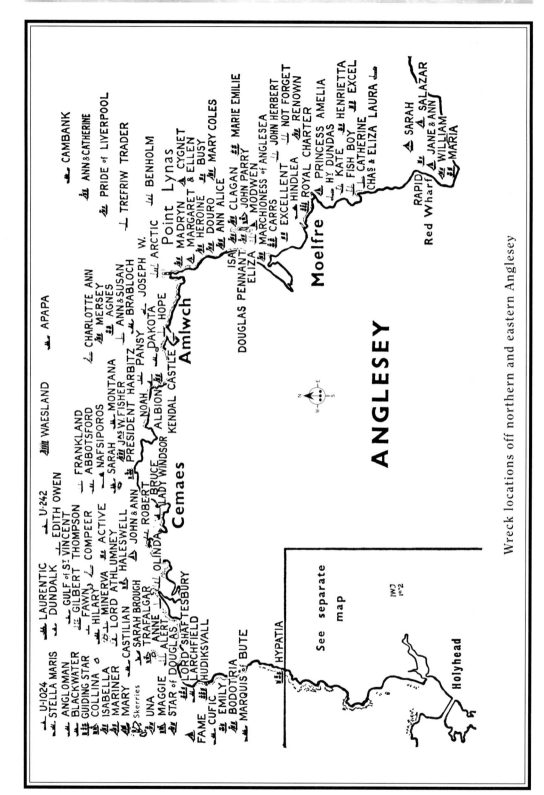

ANGLESEY

Wreck locations off northern and eastern Anglesey

of Parliament in 1730 to enforce dues of a penny per ton from British vessels and two pence per ton from foreigners. William Robinson, grandson of the man who leased out the islands, and the last of a famous family, was drowned with twelve companions while returning from the beacon on 20 June 1739. Their empty boat was washed ashore at Whitehaven, Cumberland, four days later. Morgan Jones, who inherited the 35ft-high beacon and brazier in 1778, built a new lighthouse with an oil lantern in 1804 or 1805 and bought the freehold of the Skerries in 1810. Trinity House obtained an Act of Parliament in 1836 empowering them to acquire the Skerries and nine other privately-owned lighthouses (Dungeness, Harwich, Winterton Ness, Hunstanton Cliff, Orfordness, Spurns, Tynemouth Castle, Smalls and Longships). With the refusal of successive offers the Skerries was Britain's last private lighthouse by 1841, when a special Sheriff's Court at Beaumaris fixed the purchase price at £444,984 lls 2d.

A delightful insight into the maritime habits of this remote corner of Anglesey during the eighteenth century is to be found in the diaries (preserved at the University College of North Wales, Bangor) of William Bulkeley, of Brynddu, a house still standing 1½ miles south of the little harbour of Cemaes. There, on 21 September 1742, the squire noted:

> Paid a Flintshire smuggler that was come to Cemaes from the Isle of Man 25s (£1.25) for 5 gallons of French brandy which I think is right good.

This reads in strange contrast to an entry of 14 January 1756 when the 64-years-old magistrate noted:

> Sat this day at Beaumaris to adjust the salvage due to people of Cemaes for salving 22 elephants' teeth weighing 10 cwt 2 qr and odd pounds and adjudjing them to deserve for their care and trouble 40s (£2) for every hundredweight, the teeth being valued at a median of £7 per cwt.

Other of his diary entries tell us that William Bulkeley took his daughter Mary to Dublin in 1735. There she was introduced to some excellent claret, *The Beggar's Opera* and the Liverpool privateer Fortunatus Wright, by whom she became pregnant. A hasty marriage was arranged and guests at the present-day Brynddu are shown, among other relics, Wright's sword and a picture of his brigantine *Fame* with which he captured at least sixteen French ships.

One of the most significant wrecks of all time was that of an unknown vessel which sank off Carmel Head on an unknown date between 1740 and 1745. There were only two survivors, both young boys, who came ashore lashed to a raft and speaking a strange language which prevented their rescuers from ascertaining what had happened. History has failed to record the fate of one of the boys but the other, thought to have been aged between six and eight years, and dressed in fine clothes, was placed in the care of the farmer of Maes who gave him his own name of Evan Thomas. In due course Evan acquired the Welsh tongue of his foster parents and so completely forgot his native language that in later years he was unable to determine the land of his birth although it was deduced to be Spain. As a youth Evan found that his delicate hands were gifted in the skill of bone-setting, a gift which his descendants blended with surgical training to create the internationally famous Robert Jones & Agnes Hunt Orthopaedic Hospital, near Oswestry.

Amlwch was described in 1773 as 'no more than a great chasm, between two rocks, running far into the land,' but the discovery of vast copper deposits about a mile away had made it one of the most important ports in the world. In 1793 Parliament adopted an Act 'for enlarging, deepening, cleansing, improving and regulating the harbour of Amlwch,' – the origin of the intriguing but derelict port we see today. An Amlwch schooner, the *Marchioness of Anglesea*, owned by the Mona Mine Co, was wrecked on 10 April 1818 when she was swept ashore in

The 500-ton coaster Hindlea *breaking up on the rocks near Moelfre in 1959 at almost the same point where the Royal Charter had foundered a hundred years earlier.*

Dulas Bay, three miles to the east. 'There was a great deal of plunder from the wreck before we arrived from here,' noted James Treweek, the mine agent. Of her crew of five, and twelve passengers, fourteen were drowned, the three survivors spending the night in the rigging.

The wreck of the Irish packet *Alert* on 26 March 1823 was all the more tragic for having occurred on a fine windless afternoon. Frances Williams, wife of the rector of Llan-fairynghornwy, could do nothing but seek comfort from her husband's prayers as they watched the sails of the *Alert* suddenly become limp when it rounded Carmel Head, bound for Parkgate. Gracefully and helplessly the crowded vessel drifted on to the West Mouse, less than a mile off shore. Twenty-seven bodies were recovered and buried at Holyhead and seven survivors rowed ashore, but 113 passengers vanished. If only a boat had been available to go to her aid. . . . The thought haunted Frances Williams, who established a fund to reward those who gallantly exerted themselves to save life. The nucleus of the fund – something approaching £60 – she raised by selling lithographed copies of a painting she had made in 1821 depicting the scene when George IV came ashore at Holyhead. Simultaneously Sir William Hillary, of Douglas, Isle of Man, was preparing his pamphlet which was published in 1823 under the title of: 'An appeal to the British Nation on the Humanity and Policy of Forming a National Institution for the Preservation of Lives and Property from Shipwreck,' – out of which grew what we now know as the RNLI.

When news of the formation of the institution reached the remote Anglesey rectory four years later, Frances Williams persuaded her husband to write to Col George Palmer, the lifeboat designer, pleading for one of his boats to be sent to the island. Within a month the institution had agreed and ordered a boat which was delivered on 3 November 1828, to be stationed at Cemlyn, opposite Harry's Furlong rock (sometimes described as Harry Furlough's rock), not far from the rectory. Thus Cemlyn was the first operational lifeboat station in North Wales and the inspiration for a public meeting convened by Frances Williams at the Grand Jury Room, Beaumaris, on 10 December 1828 when the Anglesey Association for the Preservation of Life from Shipwreck was formed. The Rev James Williams, husband of Frances, was the first treasurer and became secretary in 1833.

Two shipwrecks on 9 December 1830 caused a crisis in the still young Calvinistic Methodist church. The smack *Anne,* of Plymouth, carrying a general cargo, struck Harry's Furlong and went down almost immediately, although her crew managed to get to safety in their own boat. At the same time the *Active,* an Ipswich schooner, was stranded less than half-a-mile away on Cemlyn Point. Capt W. Wright and his crew were presumed to have taken to their boat but all disappeared without trace. Local elders of the Calvinistic Methodists were accused of robbing the *Active* before she broke up and the matter was hotly debated on the island. When another vessel named *Active* was wrecked in Cemaes Bay on 7 March 1835 the Rev James Williams used a horse to help him swim sufficiently near to throw a grappling hook. In this way he saved five lives and was awarded the first gold medal of the RNLI ever to go to Wales.

Point Lynas lighthouse was built by Liverpool Corporation in 1835 with an oil lantern in the ground floor of a castle-like structure atop a 128ft cliff. It replaced a light founded in 1781 with a candle and two 11in diameter polished reflectors which was exhibited from the window of a watch-house built for the Mersey pilots. It was to these pilots that the crew of the *Trefriw Trader,* a Conwy-built flat, owed their lives when their vessel sprang a leak and sank while carrying a cargo of bricks past Point Lynas on 29 April 1849. However a pilot with twenty-five years experience was blamed for the loss of the 1,130-ton iron screw steamer *Olinda,* of Liverpool, on 26 January 1854. Valued at £35,000, and only nine months old, the *Olinda* was bound for South America with a £50,000 cargo and about twenty passengers. Prevented by the weather from disembarking at Point Lynas, the pilot remained in charge and decided to take the steamer on the landward side of the Skerries. Without warning the vessel ran on to Harry's Furlong at 8.45 pm. Badly holed on the starboard side the vessel pivoted

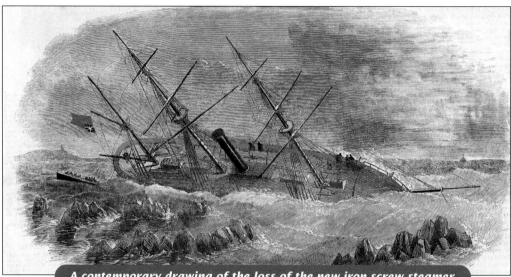

A contemporary drawing of the loss of the new iron screw steamer *Olinda* **on the Harry Furlong rocks, off Anglesey, in 1854.**

Cannon salvaged from Britain's first royal yacht, the Mary, which was found in 1971 lying in 40ft of water on the Skerries, where she sank in 1675

A contemporary artists impression of the wreck of the **Royal Charter** *near Moelfre in 1859.*

The SS Dakota, of Liverpool, was wrecked on the East Mouse, near Amlwch, on 9 May 1877. This 4,332-ton passenger liner was safely sailing for New York, in calm weather, some two miles off shore, when the 4ᵗʰ officer ordered a change of course to take her further out to sea. She mysteriously turned in the opposite direction and remained at full speed, causing her bows to rise high in the air when she hit the rocks. All her passengers and much of her cargo were saved before she fell over and sank.

The **Royal Charter** *wrecked with perhaps £500,000 in gold on board*

through 180° so that she was facing the direction from whence she came by the time the tide fell, allowing the rocks to gouge even more holes in her twisted hull. The passengers were all taken off by ship's boat or Cemlyn lifeboat and the crew were able to wade ashore at low tide. Her mail and some valuable items such as the chronometer were also taken off before the wreck was abandoned.

Outward bound from Liverpool, the SS *Arctic* was damaged when she ran aground near Point Lynas on 18 March 1854, but was able to get off under her own power and limp back to the Mersey for repairs. She belonged to the unfortunate Collins Line, of New York, which came into being in 1847 after the United States Congress decided to 'drive the Cunarders out of business'. Six months after her Point Lynas mishap, the *Arctic* sailed from Liverpool with 365 passengers, including the wife, daughter and younger son of Edward K. Collins. Seven days later, on 27 September 1854, she was rammed by the French steamer *Vesta* in thick fog off Cape Race and sank with the loss of all but fourteen passengers and thirty-four of her crew. When news of the disaster reached New York the city was draped in mourning from Bowling Green to Fourteenth Street. In 1856 her sister ship *Pacific* sailed from Liverpool with 159 passengers for New York, and vanished without trace.

The ill-fated SS *Minerva*, owned by the Cork Steam Packet Co, was wrecked on the Coal Rock, some 2½ miles ENE of the Skerries in August 1854, her crew and 130 passengers all being rescued. It was the *Minerva's* third accident. On 20 August 1850 she sliced through the brig *William Rushton* in Conwy Bay, sending it to the bottom along with seven of the crew of eleven. The *Minerva* was then a new vessel introduced on the Dublin-Liverpool run by a company specially formed to compete with the City of Dublin Steam Packet Co. On 29 March 1853 she was bound from Liverpool to Belfast when she struck and sank a vessel which was never identified north of the Calf of Man.

At least 800 lives were lost in 223 vessels wrecked on the shores of Britain during the night of 25-26 October 1859. More than half the victims had travelled 16,000 miles aboard the 719-ton luxury steam clipper *Royal Charter*, the twisted iron ribs of which may still be seen at exceptionally low tides on the northern shore of Moelfre Head. As recently as August 1970 a small brass button inscribed with the name of the Liverpool & Australian Navigation Co, owners of the *Royal Charter,* was found wedged in a crevice at the scene of the wreck. A few years before that a Conwy trawler fishing off Moelfre netted a dinner plate bearing the same inscription. When she broke up on the cliffs of Anglesey the *Royal Charter* was carrying a bullion cargo of £322,440 in gold bars or bags of dust. She may have been carrying another £150,000 in sovereigns belonging to her passengers returning home from the Australian gold field. Divers were credited with having recovered all but £30,000 worth of the bullion in the two months following the disaster, although it would seem that the salvors included in their calculations lots of sovereigns which probably belonged to passengers. The total amount of passenger gold surrendered to the Receiver of Wreck as having been found on shore or on bodies amounted to only £1,200. 'At first sovereigns had drifted in with the sand, and been scattered far and wide over the beach, like sea-shells,' wrote Charles Dickens, who visited the scene to describe the disaster in his weekly magazine *All The Year Round* – later reprinted as the first chapter of his book *The Uncommercial Traveller.* Dickens added:

> So tremendous had the force of the sea been when it broke the ship, that it had beaten one great ingot of gold deep into a strong and heavy piece of her solid iron-work: in which, also, several loose sovereigns that the ingot had swept in before it, had been found, as firmly embedded as though the iron had been liquid when they were forced there.

After four months of intensive salvage work, concentrated upon the recovery of gold, the underwriters sold the wreck for £1,000 to Gibbs, Bright & Co, of Liverpool, parent company of the original owners of the *Royal Charter.* They, in turn, continued salvage operations for two years before selling the wreck to an Anglesey consortium who worked spasmodically for another decade – and who found more than 500 sovereigns when they lifted the sternpost. With allowances for human dishonesty and tales of Anglesey folk who became mysteriously rich despite the arrival of the Militia, it is impossible to estimate how much gold still lies among the wreckage. Relics of the *Royal Charter* keep turning up in the strangest of places. A cabin door complete with doorframe was used to make the front of a cupboard which is now in a house at Llandudno, a specimen of the quality of the fittings put into the ship when she was built at Sandycroft, on the Flintshire bank of the Dee, in 1855. The ship's signal gun is on the lawn of the old Llanallgo rectory.

It is debatable whether or not the *Royal Charter* would have survived if her captain had had the courage to turn about and run for Holyhead. Capt Thomas Taylor had boasted to his first-class passengers that he would have them in Liverpool that evening, Tuesday the 25th. He was proud of his ship, his seamanship and his timekeeping and probably had no reason to suspect anything worse than Cape Horn had thrown at him so many times. By 8.00 pm, when quartermaster Owen Williams, of Caernarfon, took over the wheel, the *Royal Charter* was in serious trouble. Her gun signals for a pilot had been seen and heard from Point Lynas but no one could put out to her in a gale which was then blowing up to force 10 and veering from south-east to east-north-east. Her screw was having but little effect and there was barely any response from her rudder. Within the hour the ship was out of control and the wind was rapidly building up to force 12 – something well in excess of 75 mph. From 11.00 pm she rode to her anchors, relying upon chains made by Henry Wood & Co, of Saltney, but at 1.30 am on Wednesday the 26th the port cable snapped at the hawse hole, followed, an hour later, by the parting of the starboard cable. The great clipper slewed round to port and then raced to her doom, bows on. There were only 39 survivors, made up of 21 of her 371 passengers and 18 of her crew of 112 – the crew survivors included Thomas Griffith, a quartermaster whose home was at nearby Amlwch, and Owen Williams and Henry Evans, both of Caernarfon.

One of the passenger survivors was James Dean, a Wigan blacksmith who had spent three years seeking his fortune in the Australian gold field. While most of his fellow-passengers died rather than be parted from their heavy gold, James Dean jumped overboard and was swept ashore with his fortune intact, in the form of a banker's draft wrapped in a piece of oilskin. For the remaining thirty-six years of his life he made an annual pilgrimage to Moelfre by way of thanksgiving for his preservation and more than a century after the disaster his descendants were keeping up the tradition.

The principal memorial to the *Royal Charter's* victims is in the form of an obelisk in Llanallgo churchyard where 140 of them were buried. Forty-five were buried at Penrhoslligwy and others were buried at Llaneugrad, Llanwenllwyfo, Llanfairmathafarneithaf, Llanbedrgoch, Pentraeth, Llanddona, Amlwch and Llandudno. There is another small memorial on the cliff at the scene of the disaster.

In August 1862 Moelfre Bay was the scene of the wreck-that-never-was which cost the British taxpayer 15 1/2 million dollars compensation to the United States government. The USS *Tuscarora* had been sent to the Welsh coast to keep an eye on the steam barque *290* which was being built by Lairds, of Birkenhead, to the specifications of Confederate agent James Bulloch. It was obvious to the protesting United States ambassador that the *290* had been designed for rapid conversion into a warship and the *Tuscarora* was detailed to ensure that she never joined the Confederate navy. However the US Consul at Liverpool had no cause for alarm when the *290*, now named *Enrica*, steamed away one fine July morning. His spies had already informed him that several of Liverpool's leading citizens and their ladies had been invited aboard for the *Enrica's* first sea trials in Liverpool Bay, during which the Mersey tug *Hercules* would be standing by as a safety precaution.

Later in the day the consul was told the tug had returned, alone, her tiny deck crowded with smartly dressed women, their angry husbands and Bulloch. At first he hoped the *Enrica* had met with some disaster but before long he discovered he had fallen for the simplest of ruses. Working twenty-four hours ahead of the *Tuscarora*, Bulloch and a crew of Confederate sailors calmly made their way to Moelfre to board the *Enrica* and sail her into the Atlantic where she became the notorious CSS *Alabama*. One of her first prisoners was John Roberts whose home at Red Wharf Bay overlooked her secret anchorage of 1862. The longest-surviving ex-prisoner of the *Alabama* was Sam Roberts, of Groeslon, near Caernarfon, who died in April, 1916, aged 83.

Lifeboat stations were opened at Bull Bay in 1868, and Cemaes in 1872, so that four boats were available to rescue the crew of seventy-three when the 4,892-ton Dominion Line steamer *Angloman* struck the West Platters, in the Skerries, on 9 February 1897. The transport of live cattle from North America began in 1874 as a means of using passenger space which had been occupied by west-bound emigrants, and the *Angloman* was carrying 700 cattle and 1,500 sheep from Boston when she was wrecked, in dense fog. Soon after Cemlyn, Cemaes and two Holyhead lifeboats, assisted by the tug *William Jolliffe,* had taken off all the men the steamer slipped off the rocks and sank. Six months later the wreck was sold in situ for £115 and can still be seen by divers, lying in about 35ft of water.

The White Star liner *Cufic* was abandoned when dangerously near the Skerries on 20 December 1900. Having developed engine trouble in the Irish Sea, she was being towed to Liverpool by two tugs when the tow lines snapped, leaving the ship to the mercy of a 50 mph south-westerly gale. Both anchors were dropped but the *Cufic* was within a few feet of disaster before they became effective, and although the anchors held this seemed most unlikely when the entire crew of forty-one were taken off by Holyhead lifeboat. There was another towing mishap in 1901 when the 1,000-ton iron barque *Gilbert Thompson* drifted slightly to starboard and struck the West Mouse. All the crew, except a cabin boy, were rescued after jumping on to the rock before the vessel sank.

Built and registered at Peel, the schooner **Kate** was Amlwch-owned. She spent most of her time in the Cornish china-clay trade, and was sailing from Cornwall to Runcorn on 31 January 1933 when she took shelter in Moelfre Roads. There a fire broke out in one of the cabins and the crew of four was rescued by Moelfre lifeboat. She burnt down to the waterline and sank.

The schooner **Lily**, of Padstow, was carrying coal from Runcorn, when driven onto the West Mouse, near Cemlyn, and wrecked, on 18 October 1907.

Many vessels, and many more sailors, have ended their days on Dulas Island which is the foul-smelling visible third of a treacherous reef half-a-mile offshore in Dulas Bay. So as to make the hazard more obvious James Hughes built a tower on the island in 1824 but was sufficiently pessimistic to incorporate a fireplace and fire-making materials for the comfort of the shipwrecked. Three-quarters of a century later Lady (Dorina) Neave, whose home overlooked the bay, kept the tower stocked with food and had the pleasure of seeing it put to good use several times. One of the Dulas Island wrecks of the beginning of the last century is still described as *y llong y wlanen goch,* which is Welsh for 'the red flannel ship,' in reference to her cargo. The *John Parry,* a Bangor schooner, was wrecked there on 9 December 1902. Another wreck of the same period was the *Eliza,* of Inverness, whose master was a Moelfre man. Capt Richard Owen, second coxswain of Moelfre lifeboat, and an RNLI silver medallist, was marooned on the island when the yacht *Modwen,* which he was skippering, ran aground at about the same time.

The early years of the twentieth century produced a batch of collisions near the Skerries. The Glasgow-registered steamer *Stella Maris* sank immediately after being struck by the Spanish steamship *Oria,* two miles west of the Skerries, on 7 January 1905. All the crew were picked up in the dark by the *Oria* but she, too, was badly damaged and later sank 500yd from the end of Holyhead breakwater where both crews took to the *Oria's* two boats – one of which was equipped with but a single oar. The steamer *Blackwater,* on passage from Dublin to Liverpool, sank in similar circumstances and much the same location after a collision with the SS *Wexford* on 10 July 1905 – her crew of twelve being saved by the latter ship. Ten days later the *Sarah Brough,* in ballast from Dublin and bound for Llanddulas, first holed herself on the Skerries and then sank on the West Mouse, her crew saving themselves.

A torpedo from the *U-30* sank the 3,112-ton SS *Cambank,* of Cardiff, nearly five miles east-by-north-east of Point Lynas, on 20 February 1915. Her crew of twenty-one were rescued by Bull Bay lifeboat and some of her copper cargo was raised during the 1950s. HMS *Pansy,* a 333-ton Wallasey ferry paddle steamer which had been requisitioned by the Admiralty, sank in protest when subjected to a north-easterly gale off Bull Bay in 1916. Her wreckage was found by amateur divers in 1968, lying in fairly shallow water a third of a mile offshore at the western end of the bay. Wartime lighting restrictions caused the sinking of the Barrow schooner *Clagan* on Dulas Island on 28 June 1917, with the loss of all but the cabin boy who scrambled ashore accompanied by the ship's dog. Another war casualty was the 7,832-ton armed merchant ship *Apapa* which was sunk NNW of Point Lynas while returning from West Africa on 28 November 1917.

One of the many wrecks rotting off Point Lynas is the humble auxiliary ketch *Excel* which sank on 28 October 1927 amid a display of the heroism which has characterised Moelfre lifeboat station ever since its foundation in 1830. The waterlogged ketch was about 3¹/₂ miles north-east of the lighthouse when the ten-oar lifeboat *Charles & Eliza Laura* found her in a whole gale. A German freighter which had taken the *Excel* in tow cut her adrift at the approach of the lifeboat and Coxswain William Roberts, after consultation with crew-man Capt Owen Jones, decided to sail over the sinking bows of the ketch. During this desperate manoeuvre the three-man crew of the *Excel* were hauled to safety but not before the hull of the lifeboat had been shattered from below by two violent blows athwart the ketch. Thirteen hours later the shocked and exhausted crew, kept afloat only by their air cases, managed to get near enough to Puffin Island to anchor. By the time Beaumaris motor lifeboat reached them one of the Moelfre men and one of the crew of the *Excel* were dead. Gold medals were awarded to the coxswain and to the master mariner who had taken the place of a sick crew-man, and bronze medals went to the rest of the crew.

Damaged beyond repair the *Charles & Eliza Laura* was replaced by the lifeboat *Henry Dundas* which had served at St Mary's, in the Scilly Isles, from 1899 to 1919, and then at

Angle, Milford Haven, until transferred to Moelfre. She was wrecked on the Moelfre shore after breaking away from her moorings on 11 February 1929, Coxswain John Matthews receiving the RNLI silver medal for devotion to duty during the incident. The closing chapter in the story of the *Excel* occurred during August 1932 when Capt Owen Jones, the gold medallist, vanished with his fishing-boat somewhere between Point Lynas and the Great Orme.

With the burning of the sixty-one-year-old Isle of Man-built schooner *Kate*, of Amlwch, in Moelfre Bay during January 1933, the sailing history of Anglesey's copper creek came to an end. Another interesting schooner which required the services of Moelfre lifeboat on 16 November 1934 was the *Marie Celine,* built at Nantes in 1892. After a remarkable series of mishaps she had by this time been re-rigged as a ketch and sported an auxiliary motor. With the aid of lifeboatmen, who were put on board, the *Marie Celine* was towed to safety.

Six were killed outright and several were seriously injured when the Maier-form bows of the *Napier Star,* a 10,500-ton Blue Star cargo ship, chopped through the crew's quarters of the White Star passenger liner *Laurentic* north of the Skerries at 3.00 am on 18 August 1935. The 18,700-ton *Laurentic* was only a couple of hours out of Liverpool with 600 passengers booked for a fourteen-day Scandinavian cruise. In dense fog men and women wearing night clothes assembled at boat stations but later were allowed to return to their cabins while the ship limped back to the Gladstone Dock. Shipwrights and a medical team met the *Laurentic* at the Mersey Bar where they took two hours to release the dead and the injured from the grotesquely twisted steel. Built in 1927, the *Laurentic* was the world's last transatlantic passenger liner either to be fired by coal or to be engined with reciprocating machinery. She was sunk in the North Western approaches by a torpedo fired from the *U-99* on 3 November 1940.

The last passenger ship mishap on this coast involved the 7,400-ton Booth liner *Hilary* which ran on to the Coal Rock while homeward bound from Brazil on 9 April 1939. After searching in thick fog Holyhead lifeboat found the ship firmly aground and took off 84 of her 300 passengers. When they returned for more of her passengers the lifeboat crew found the liner was beginning to refloat on the rising tide. The *Hilary* eventually got off under her own power and continued her voyage to Liverpool.

The wartime blackout of the Skerries light resulted in the loss of the 3,067-ton Ellerman Lines steamship *Castilian* on 12 February 1943. Her anchors had failed to hold her against a south-westerly gale in Church Bay and the master decided to steam north out of harm's way. He ran on to the East Platters, forming part of the Skerries, and was firmly wedged when located by Holyhead lifeboat. Coxswain Richard Jones and Mechanic John Jones were awarded the RNLI bronze medal for their skill and perseverence in repeatedly bringing the lifeboat alongside the *Castilian* until all forty-seven members of the crew had jumped to safety. That afternoon the ship slipped into over 100ft of water, where she still lies with her cargo of copper ore and explosives.

In the closing weeks of World War II three German submarines were reported sunk north-west of Anglesey. The *U-1024* was blown to the surface midway between Holyhead and Dublin with a single squid pattern of depth charges fired from the frigate HMS *Loch Glendhu*, late on the evening of 10 April 1945. A boarding party was sent out and the U-boat was taken in tow by HMS *Loch More*. Some twenty-four hours later the tow parted and the U-boat sank. On the last day of April a Sunderland flying-boat of 201 Squadron, RAF, sighted a *schnorkel* some twenty miles north-west of the Skerries and called up the destroyers HMS *Hesperus* and HMS *Havelock*. The subsequent depth charge attack was assumed to have accounted for both the *U-242* and *U-325* although in a footnote to his official history, *The War at Sea,* Capt S. W. Roskill said in 1961 that the original post-war assessment of the fate of the *U-325* 'is probably incorrect.'

However it is in peacetime that this troubled shore has produced its greatest dramas, such as the destruction of the *Hindlea* on 27 October 1959 – less than twenty-four hours after a special evening service at Llanallgo church to commemorate the centenary of the sinking of the *Royal Charter*. As a southwesterly gale unexpectedly veered to north Richard Evans, coxswain of Moelfre lifeboat, received a telephone message from Holyhead coastguard headquarters telling him a 500-ton coaster which had been sheltering in Dulas Bay had started to drag her anchor. His knowledge of what had happened in identical circumstances a hundred years earlier told Mr Evans that the *Hindlea* was doomed. There was no time even to collect his full crew if the men aboard the coaster were to be saved and he put to sea with mechanic Evan Owens, two of his crew and volunteer Hugh Jones who had never been out in a lifeboat before. Just to complicate matters none of them had been out in the *Edmund & Mary Robinson*, a reserve lifeboat which had been sent to Moelfre while their own 42ft boat, the *Watkin Williams*, was undergoing a refit.

Riding 25ft waves through a 104 mph hurricane they found the *Hindlea* rolling violently on one cable, her screw racing out of the water more than it was in. For nearly one and a half hours the master delayed the command to abandon ship, with the result that she was only about 200yd off shore when the inevitable signal was given. As the lifeboat rode into the intervening cauldron anxious shore watchers saw her thrown onto her beam ends until the mast was under water, but the *Edmund & Mary Robinson* came up in one piece and after withdrawing to reassess the situation Coxswain Evans again rode in for a trial run on the *Hindlea's* port quarter. This time the lifeboat was hurled against the ship with such force that everyone thought she must be seriously damaged. Undaunted, Coxswain Evans repeated the manoeuvre another eight times and on each occasion a member of the crew of the *Hindlea* jumped to safety. Soon afterwards the coaster, which had been in ballast from Manchester to Newport, was hurled against the cliffs with a fury which broke her in two.

For this spectacular service Coxswain Evans received the RNLI gold medal, Mechanic Owens received the silver, and the three others received the bronze. Seven years later Coxswain Evans achieved the rare distinction of being awarded a second gold medal for rescuing ten men from the Greek freighter *Nafsiporos* off the West Mouse during the evening of 2 December 1966. Five more of the crew were taken off by the Holyhead lifeboat *St Cybi*, temporarily under the command of ex-Fleet Air Arm Lt-Cdr Harold Harvey, RNLI district inspector, who also received the gold medal.

Running empty to Liverpool the 1,287-ton *Nafsiporos* was riding so high that her screw was having little effect against a northerly 110 mph hurricane. Answering the 'mayday' appeal for help of Capt Katsoufis, the Russian timber ship *Kungerlees* had managed to get a tow line across but it snapped when both vessels were perilously near Ethel Rock, north of Carmel Head. The *Nafsiporos* had already lost one anchor in the struggle and disaster on the West Mouse seemed imminent when the lifeboats moved in. Capt Katsoufis and three of his men remained on board in anticipation of the arrival of the Dutch salvage tug *Utrecht* and after a prolonged radio debate over terms the *Nafsiporos* was towed to Liverpool.

The most recent wrecks on this coast have been small boats belonging to a Liverpool team of divers, who set up camp on the Moelfre cliffs in the spring of 1985. Their boats were mysteriously sabotaged when, after diving for several weeks, they let it be known they were bringing up gold from the *Royal Charter*. Using modern techniques to remove several feet of silt clogging up most of the 126-year-old wreck, they began recovering Australian-minted sovereigns, and a variety of artefacts including jewellery, a solid gold bottom denture, the gold hilt of a dagger and a gold button from the captain's tunic. Dismissing contemporary estimates of the gold abandoned by the original salvors, the 1985 team said they were hoping to find gold now worth £5,000,000. Earlier divers had been diverted from the main wreckage, lying in only 25ft of water, by concentrating their efforts on the more readily identifiable deck which had been torn away from the rest of the ship during a 1905 treasure-hunt.

IN the days when the bulk of British transport relied upon small sailing vessels, the Menai Strait presented an attractive alternative to the long and hazardous haul around northwest Anglesey. An almost straight short-cut, twelve miles long and nowhere less than 250yd wide, it looked like a haven compared with the cruel coast traversed in previous chapters. For landsmen, however, the Menai Strait has always been a treacherous barrier necessitating the use of ferries with an unenviable record of disaster.

This was the setting for the first known defeat of the Royal Navy when, off Tal-y-foel in 1157, the forces of Owain Gwynedd, Prince of North Wales, defeated the combined English, Irish and Danish fleet of King Henry II. It was 1284 before the English got their final revenge, annexing Wales and building enormous castles at Caernarfon and Conwy (followed by another at Beaumaris) at opposite ends of the Menai Strait.

A dispute over a penny caused the first ferry disaster of which we have a record. It happened in 1664 on the Abermenai ferry which had been established by Edward I to ply the two miles from Caernarfon to the southernmost tip of Newborough Warren. The ferryboat had arrived at its Anglesey destination, the oars had been stowed and the eighty people on board were on their feet ready to disembark when a dispute arose over the fare. Slowly the boat drifted into deep water where it was seized by the tide spilling through the narrow exit to the sea. Suddenly it capsized and sank along with seventy-nine of the passengers. When the lone survivor told his story the people of Newborough attributed the disaster to heavenly wrath consequent upon the ferry boat's having been made of wood stolen from the disused Llanddwyn church.

Moel-y-don ferry, another creation of Edward I, operated from what is now Port Dinorwig, midway aglong the Strait and was maintained as a Crown ferry until as recently as October 1935. This ferryboat sank on 6 October 1710 while carrying fifteen men and ten horses. They were near the Caernarvonshire shore at the time and all the passengers were saved. The sinking was due to a particularly rough sea affecting the whole of the Strait. At the western end Abermenai ferryboat was forced to abandon an attempt to leave Caernarfon, while in between a boat belonging to Mr H. Evans, of Llanidan, was sunk while trying to return to Anglesey from Caernarfon.

Tal-y-foel ferry originated as a direct crossing from Caernarfon, the Strait being a mile wide at this point. Crown rights were sold to Caernarfon Corporation in 1874 from which date the Anglesey landing place was moved nearly a mile to the east to remain in use until 30 July 1954. Thirty people were drowned when the ferryboat capsized on 13 April 1723. Two survived the disaster, a man who clung to the upturned keel and a boy who grabbed the tail of a horse which managed to swim ashore.

Abermenai ferry was involved in a particularly sad disaster on 5 December 1785. It was a fair day at Caernarfon and there were fifty-five people on board when the boat left the town at 4.00 pm, about an hour before low water. All would have been well if the boat had kept to the channel but when about a mile from town she grounded on one of the sandbanks which dry out in the middle of the Strait at low tide. Passengers joined in repeated efforts to relaunch

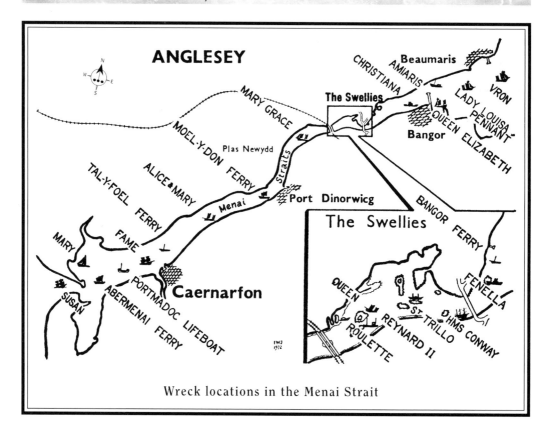

Wreck locations in the Menai Strait

the heavy boat but the wind was against them and the vessel filled with water and sank. This left fifty-five men, women and children marooned on a sandbank which would become submerged with the incoming tide. Their united cries for help were heard on shore and several boats went to investigate, including the Caernarfon customs boat and a Barmouth sloop which had been riding at anchor. Tragically, the gentle slope of the sandbank and shallow approaches prevented any vessel from getting near enough to be of assistance and the stranded people realised that they were doomed. As the tide rose, they died gradually, in ones and twos or as families. Parents were faced with the agonising choice of prolonging the suffering of their children by lifting them out of the rising water or of deliberately dropping them into the sea as their own strength gave way. One man survived to described the horror. He was Hugh Williams, of Ty'n Llwydan, a house which still overlooks Aberffraw Bay. He swam for two hours with the aid of the boat's mast and an oar which he had tied together, and came ashore near Tal-y-foel ferry house. By a strange coincidence a man named Hugh Williams was the only survivor when the Tal-y-foel ferryboat sank in 1820, also on 5 December. On that occasion twenty-five people were drowned, due to what was said to be too much sail and overloading on a windy day.

Caernarfon's principal harbour has always been the sheltered estuary of the River Seiont, which was greatly improved by a scheme launched in 1817 to reclaim the extensive area known ever since as the Slate Quay. It was built to handle the output from the quarries of the Nantlle Valley which, from 1828, were linked to Caernarfon by a railway. At the opposite end of the Menai Strait the conversion of Abercegin creek into Port Penrhyn began in 1790 simultaneously with the development of the Bethesda slate quarries. Midway between Caernarfon and Bangor the owners of the Llanberis quarries created Port Dinorwig in 1824.

Thus, instead of being a shortcut to or from the Dee and the Mersey, the Menai Strait began to generate a whole new maritime economy of its own.

Being heavy in relation to their bulk, a valuable cargo of Caernarvonshire slates left a lot of empty space in the holds, space which wily shipowners sold to emigrants. 'If any of you are for coming here, take care not to come with slates from Caernarfon,' warned Dafydd Shone Harry, writing from America to his family at Llwyngwril, Merioneth, in 1817. It was a warning which thousands of Welshmen ignored and a poster typical of the Welsh scene of the period is displayed at Caernarfon public library:

> **For New York. Direct.**
> The fine fast sailing barque *Hindoo*, of Caernarvon, burthen about 600 tons (the sole property of Mr H. Owen, Rhyddgar, Anglesey), Richard Hughes, Commander, will be ready to sail from this port on or about the middle of March next with a ballast of slates. Emigrants will find this conveyance most convenient for embarking for the United States, the vessel being properly fitted out for the accommodation of passengers. For freight and passage, and further particulars, an early application is requested to be made to the Commander on board, or to John Owen, High Street.
> Caernarvon
> 1st Feb 1843.

The terms were £10 per family, the passengers to provide their own food and bedding, the *Hindoo* to provide water, fuel and sleeping space. The words 'being properly fitted out for the accommodation of passengers' simply meant that the slates would be so stacked as to provide bays which the emigrants could occupy for anything between six and ten weeks.

Caernarfon Bar had long been recognised as a major navigational hazard but many vessels crossed it in safety only to find other dangers. Some ran aground on Abermenai Point, like *Susan*, a London brig, in 1833, or the *Mary*, a Waterford sloop, in 1834. Some entered the Strait but were wrecked on the shifting sandbanks opposite Caernarfon. Four went aground on these sandbanks on a single day in 1836. Three broke up but the fourth, a Bridgewater brig named *Fame*, was towed into Caernarfon where she remained for many a month with her bowsprit reaching out over the road at the junction of Bank Quay and Balaclava Road – a reminder that the area known as Turkey Shore really was a shore before the reclamation of the land to make the patent slip leading into the 'new basin' or Victoria Dock during 1868-71. The Strait was not immune to storms, a vessel named the *Queen Elizabeth* being wrecked at Bangor during the '*Royal Charter* gale' in 1859. The Swellies, a swirling mass of rock-strewn water, claimed the *Queen*, a Caernarfon smack, in 1864. A Bangor smack, the *Alice & Mary*, was lost in the Swellies in 1869, and another Bangor smack, the *Mary Grace*, was lost in a collision in the Strait in 1874. The *Vron*, a Nefyn schooner of 101 tons, disappeared without trace after sailing out of Bangor on 17 December 1880.

The bridging of the Menai Strait, first mooted in 1783, became a fact in 1826 when Thomas Telford completed his famous suspension bridge – complying with the Admiralty requirement for 100ft clearance above spring tides. In 1850 Britannia Rock gave its name to the ingenious Britannia Tubular Bridge which Robert Stephenson built to complete the London-Holyhead rail link. Seriously damaged by fire on 23 May 1970, the Britannia Bridge has since been replaced by an arched span bridge with 90ft clearance at the centre – a design rejected by the Admiralty as a navigational hazard when first put forward by Robert Stephenson during the original planning of the railway.

The Anglesey township of Menai Bridge, named after the suspension bridge which runs into it, soon became a popular tourist centre for steamer trips from as far afield as Blackpool. It was at the end of one such trip that the 564-ton twin-screw steamer *Fenella*, owned by the

Isle of Man Steam Packet Co, was badly holed on 9 September 1884. Carrying about a hundred day excursionists from Douglas, the *Fenella* took on a pilot at Penmon but his duties ended when he crossed Garth Ferry, two miles short of Menai Bridge. Thereafter the captain, making his first visit to the Strait, was on his own. Immediately after disembarking his passengers at the pier he had to make way for the paddle-steamer *Bonnie Princess,* owned by the Liverpool, Llandudno & Welsh Coast Steamboat Co. It was a manoeuvre requiring him to turn his ship between shores 300yd apart. During this operation the *Fenella* drifted broadside on to Half-tide Rock, midway between the pier and the suspension bridge, which is submerged at high tide. 'The rock is not buoyed and within the last two years more than one schooner has run on her,' admonished the *Holyhead & Anglesey Mail* adding: 'The casualty will probably hasten the carrying into effect of what has long been felt necessary.'

As the tide fell so the *Fenella* dropped lower onto the rock which trapped her, at the same time rolling away from the rock. Her anchors were deployed to hold her and she was straining at the chains at an angle of 45°, with two holes clearly visible in her hull, by the time the tide was at its lowest at 7.30 pm. With her holes temporarily plugged the *Fenella* was refloated, and towed off at midnight by the 97-ton screw steamer *Satanella,* the only vessel owned by the Bangor, Beaumaris & Llandudno Steam Packet Co Ltd, and was beached at Cae Coch on the Caernarvonshire shore. After being repaired, the *Fenella* continued to serve the company until 1929 when she was broken up at Newport. A second ship of the same name was sunk at Dunkirk on 30 May 1940, but was salvaged by the Germans and renamed the *Reval,* later to be captured by the Russians. Undaunted, the Isle of Man Steam Packet Co gave the name to yet a third ship in 1951.

Anxious to syphon off some of the trippers sailing past them to Menai Bridge in ever-increasing numbers, Bangor City Council built a pier in 1896. It stretched for 1,550ft along the route of the old Garth Ferry, being more than half the width of the Strait at this point. Most of the material for the construction of the pier was carried in the Liverpool steam coaster *Christiana* which plied up and down the Menai Strait for many years. Her first master was Capt John J. Griffith who was born into a seafaring family at Penmaen Pool in 1853. His remarkable career included command of the 298-ton Porthmadog barque *Pride of Wales* which he was forced to abandon in the Atlantic in 1893. After that he decided to confine his sailing to the coasting trade and was in command of the Liverpool-Caernarfon steamer *Ibis* when she was sunk in a collision off New Brighton. His third mishap was with the *Christiana* at the turn of the century. Caught by a storm after leaving Beaumaris for Liverpool, he turned back to seek shelter at Menai Bridge. There the vessel was struck by a cross-wind and driven on to the Caernarvonshire shore where her propeller was smashed. After being lifted off by the tide, the *Christiana* was blown all the way back to Bangor pier which she struck at the shore end, close to the old cargo landing stage of which there is no longer any trace. Both the pier and the vessel which had helped to build it were extensively damaged.

Two slate-carrying schooners vanished after leaving Port Penrhyn on 14 October 1902 and it is conjectured that they may have collided with each other. They were the *Fomalhaut,* built at Bangor in 1874, and the veteran *Lady Louisa Pennant* built in 1847, also at Bangor.

One of the pleasure steamers of the Liverpool & North Wales Steamship Co ran onto a rock in the Swellies on 14 July 1921. She was the 198-ton *St Trillo* which was returning from a trip to Caernarfon with some 200 passengers. Immediately after she struck the *St Trillo* heeled over and only those who have witnessed the speed with which the water races through these dreaded rocks can appreciate the fear which spread among the passengers. All were ordered to wear lifejackets and distress signals were made. Local motor boats were the first to respond and took off small groups of passengers. Later the paddle steamer *Snowdon,* belonging to the owners of the *St Trillo,* and the visiting Blackpool paddle-steamer *Greyhound,* also joined in the rescue operation. With a rising tide the *St Trillo* suddenly slipped into deep

HMS Conway *at Bangor Pier*

water throwing the cook overboard and causing a moment or two of panic among the passengers still on board. A member of the crew jumped over the side to save the cook and after both had been hauled back on board the *St Trillo* sailed to Port Dinorwig where she was put into dock. At the end of the summer she was sold to a Spanish owner and re-named *San Telmo*. When launched in 1876 she was named the *Carisbrooke* but was re-named *Rhos Trevor* in 1906, and *St Trillo* in 1909, serving as the minesweeper HMS *St Trillo* during l9l4-l8. She ended her career as a floating hotel for Spanish duck-shooting expeditions and was removed from the registers in 1931.

Probably the most famous of all the Menai Strait shipwrecks was that of the former 92-gun warship HMS *Conway* on 14 April 1953, watched by hundreds of people gathered on the Menai suspension bridge. The *Conway* was laid down at Devonport in October 1827 and was launched as HMS *Nile* in June 1839. She was 240ft long, 53ft wide and her weight was given as 2,622 tons burthen (1791 formula) which became 4,375 tons under the 1834 formula. However Britain was at peace and the *Nile* was never commissioned as a sailing ship. She remained an unfinished hull until 1852 when she was docked to be fitted with steam engines and a propeller. It was April of 1854, twenty-seven years after being laid down, before the *Nile* joined the Navy to be sent to the Gulf of Finland where Britain was blockading the Russian fleet. Her first visit to the Mersey was in 1859 when she moored off Rock Ferry close to the frigate HMS *Conway*, which had just arrived on loan from the Admiralty to the Mercantile Marine Service Association for use as a cadet school for Merchant Navy officers. Stripped of her engines the *Nile* returned to the Mersey on 23 June 1876 to become the third training ship to bear the proud name of HMS *Conway*. She remained at the Sloyne, off the Cheshire shore, until 22 May 1941 when, because of heavy air raids, she was evacuated to a berth near Bangor pier which had been occupied for many years by another wooden training vessel, the corvette HMS *Clio*.

**Four views of HMS Conway *after running aground.
She was an incalculable loss to Britain's naval heritage.***

The training ship HMS Conway *a few hours after drifting ashore in the Menai Strait and before she broke her back.*

Instead of moving their ship back to the Mersey after the war, the MMSA set about seeking an anchorage which would also provide a shore-base in close proximity, the choice finally falling upon Plas Newydd, an eighteenth-century mansion belonging to the Marquess of Anglesey. After a careful survey of the five miles of the Menai Strait separating Plas Newydd from Bangor pier it was agreed that the new tenants should move in with the spring tides of April 1949. With a draft of 22ft the *Conway* was the biggest vessel ever to pass through the Swellies. The two Caernarfon pilots, Mr R. J. Jones and his son Mr J. R. Jones, took charge of the operation using two Liverpool tugs, the *Dongarth* ahead and the *Minegarth* aft. After a twenty-four hour delay because of winds the tow was carried out on 13 April. There were some anxious moments when it was found that the tow had taken ten minutes more than predicted to reach the suspension bridge. The greatest of all the hazards in the Swellies is the swift and violent tidal change arising out of the time gap between the rise or fall at opposite ends of the Strait. Now working behind schedule, the *Conway* went through on the turbulent ebb, passing within 5ft of Gorad Goch Island, before reaching the safe water beyond the tubular bridge.

Caught in the treacherous turn of the tide race while being towed through the Menai Strait in 1953, the 92-gun screw ship Conway, **launched in 1839 as the** Nile, **broke adrift and was declared a total loss within 24 hours.**

Four years later it was proposed to reverse the process to enable the *Conway* to be put into dry-dock at Birkenhead for a refit. On the eve of the tow Mr R. J. Jones, the senior pilot, told the author that he had asked for three tugs so as to have a safety margin in the event of some unforeseen contingency in the carefully-timed schedule. His request had been turned down on the basis of the 1949 tow having been successful – and he was supplied with the same two tugs to ensure a carbon-copy operation. The strange trio set out on the morning of 14 April 1953 and, as in the case of the original tow, they were a few minutes late entering the Swellies. They were almost through, with the lead tug nearly under the watching crowd on the suspension bridge, when they were gripped in the full force of the ebb and brought to a standstill. Slowly they began to drift astern, a movement which was temporarily counteracted by bringing the rear tug up to the front. Suddenly the towing line connecting the two tugs snapped and the old *Conway* gracefully gathered speed, towing the remaining tug with her. She beached on the Caernarvonshire shore, close to the suspension bridge, and within a few hours it was obvious to all that she had broken her back. On April 15 the *Conway* was declared a total loss and three years later the wreck was destroyed by fire.

HMS *Conway* lived on for some years at Plas Newydd, full of misplaced confidence in Britain's maritime future. A luxurious new shore establishment, with accommodation for 316 cadets, was opened by Prince Philip on 4 May 1964, but just a decade later the school was scuttled. During her 115 years she had produced four VCs, more than 30 flag officers, several bishops, a poet laureate and the captains of every British transatlantic liner except the *Titanic*. She also produced several of the senior officers for the Falkland Islands War, in 1982, including Vice-Admiral D. W. Brown, Assistant Chief of Defence Staff (Operations), Rear Admiral J. P. Edwards, Deputy Chief of Fleet Support, Captain A. P. Woodhead, RN, Chief of Staff with the Task Force, Captain G. R. Green, who received the DSC as master of the RFA *Sir Tristram*, Captain C. G. Butterworth, Marine Superintendent RFA, and the masters of the *Fort Grange, Europic Ferry, Geestport, Baltic Ferry, Avelona Star, Lycaon, Tidespring* and *British Dart*, two of whom received OBEs.

At Plas Llanfair, another old family seat of the Marquesses of Anglesey, a mile nearer to the Britannia bridge, the TS *Indefatigable* National Sea Training School for Boys has been a shore establishment since 1944, having been founded in 1864 in the frigate HMS *Indefatigable* anchored close to the *Conway* in the Mersey.

Here lies the body
of John Tarrey of
Bury. Lancashire.
Aged 2 Years.
who lost his life in the
Rothsay Castle.
on the 18th of August.
1831.

The tombstone at Llansanffraid Glan Conwy of two-years-old John Tarrey who was swept up the River Conwy after the Rothsay Castle disaster. His mother Alice is buried on the Great Orme, at Llandudno.

CONWY BAY

CONWY river and bay derive their name from the dismay of the ancient Britons who arrived at Deganwy, on the right bank, and called the obstacle before them Cyn-gwy, meaning Big Water. The river crossing into the mountain fastnesses of Snowdonia remained a formidable and frequently lethal problem until it was bridged by Thomas Telford in 1826; the sea crossing to Anglesey still involved nine miles of skilful navigation. Between the two alternatives lies the mouth of the Menai Strait, separating Caernarvonshire and Anglesey, while the northern mouth of the bay is guarded by two treacherous headlands, the Great Orme in the east and Puffin Island in the west.

Anxious to subdue the Celts of Anglesey, Julius Agricola, Roman governor of Britain, created another alternative when he arrived with his Twentieth Legion in the year 77. He went seven miles up river to find a ford, established a left-bank bridgehead called Canovium, being the latinised version of Cyn-gwy, and struck out across the mountains to Aber where, at low tide, the Lavan Sands form a natural three-mile pier reaching towards Anglesey.

'The plan was hastily conceived,' wrote his son-in-law Tacitus. 'No fleet was available and the ingenuity of the general had to take the troops across. Agricola selected the best of his troops, with experience of fords and who had been trained at home to swim with their horses beside them,' he added. In this way the quarter-mile channel was crossed at slack water and the whole of Wales was absorbed within the Roman Empire.

Much of the subsequent history of Wales centres around the political or military solutions to the barrier of the Conwy and it is within this context that we read of our first recorded shipwreck here on Monday 24 September 1245. England and Wales were at war and King Henry III and his army were camped at Deganwy, besieged, cold and hungry. One of the royal household described the scene:

> There is a small arm of the sea which ebbs and flows under the aforesaid castle (where we are staying) and forming a sort of harbour into which, during our stay here, ships have often come from Ireland and from Chester, bringing provisions. This arm of the sea lies between us and Snowdon, where the Welsh quarter themselves, and is, at high tide, about a crossbow-shot wide. On the Monday next before Michaelmas, in the afternoon, a ship from Ireland, bringing provisions to us for sale, was coming up towards the entrance of the harbour, but being incautiously steered, as the sea receded it remained aground under our aforesaid castle, but on the opposite bank, towards the Welsh, who immediately rushed down and made an attack on it as it lay on the dry ground.

The un-named vessel was firmly aground on what we now call Conwy Morfa. Desperate for the food contained in her the king sent an expedition of crossbowmen and dismounted knights across the river, using boats manned by Borderland mercenaries. Deceived by the Welsh, who made a tactical retreat, the English raiding party plundered the nearby Cistercian abbey, burial place of Llewelyn the Great, and then set it on fire. The chronicle continues:

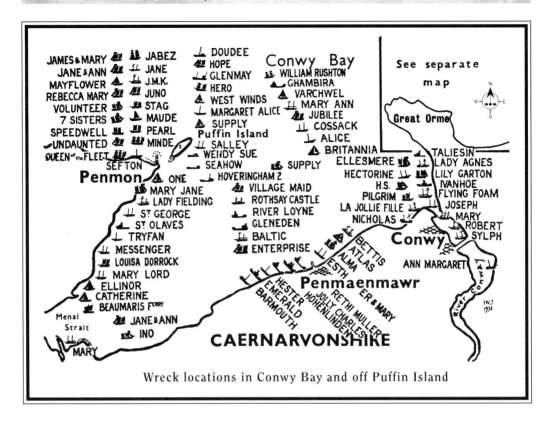

Wreck locations in Conwy Bay and off Puffin Island

The Welsh, in the meantime having assembled a great host of their countrymen, suddenly rushed with noisy shouts on our men, who were laden with booty acquired by the most wicked means, and who were impeded by their sins, and put them to flight, wounding and slaying many as they retreated towards the ship; some of our people choosing rather to trust to the mercy of the waves, and to perish by drowning, than to be slain at will by their enemies, threw themselves of their own accord into the waves, there to perish. Some of our knights they took alive, to imprison them; but hearing that we had slain some of their nobles, and above all Nefydd, son of Odo, a handsome and brave youth, they also hanged these knights of ours, later decapitating and mangling them dreadfully; finally they tore their miserable corpses limb from limb, and threw them into the water, in detestation of their wicked greediness in not sparing the church.

Sir Walter Bissett and some of his knights succeeded in defending the ship until the incoming tide and the darkness ended the Welsh attack.

On board this ship were sixty casks of wine, besides other much-desired and seasonable provisions of which we were at the time destitute. When morning came, and the tide receded, the Welsh returned with alacrity, thinking to seize on our people in the vessel but, by God's providence, they had, during the night when the tide was high, made their escape to us by means of our boats, before the arrival of the Welsh, leaving only the ship. The Welsh, however, approached, carried off nearly all the wine and other things on board, and leaving the ship as the tide rose, set fire to the vessel, a portion of which was consumed; the other part, however, was saved, in which were seven casks which we dragged to the near shore.

Thirty-eight years later the English finally crossed the Conwy, created the town and fortress of the same name on the site of the Cistercian abbey, and established the Port of Beaumaris which really means Conwy Bay and whose registration letters 'BS' are still used for vessels based upon the natural harbour at Conwy (where the present quay wall was built in 1835).

Our earliest named wreck in this bay is the *Nicholas,* of Carne, whose master was Nicholas Cushen when she was cast ashore on the Morfa in 1576 while carrying a cargo of corn destined for Normandy. A Spanish spy who had a look at the bay at this time, in anticipation of the troubles which led to the sailing and the defeat of the Armada of 1588, noted that there was room for a hundred ships at the Port of Beaumaris, adding that the people here 'speak a language apart' in reference to the Welsh language which is still very much a part of the daily life on the shores of Conwy Bay.

Puffin Island, which also has the names of Priestholm or the Welsh Ynys Seiriol (meaning St Seiriol's Island), is a 67-acre hump of rock three-fifths of a mile long and a fifth wide. It stands a quarter of a mile off the extreme eastern tip of Anglesey. On the 163ft high summit there is a tower, the remains of a religious establishment of uncertain antiquity, while on the northern tip there is the shell of one of the Liverpool semaphore stations. Somewhere among the dense growth which covers the top of the island there is also a tombstone bearing the crudely carved inscription: 'Bar^e. Stout belonging to the *Salley* died in the small pox Novr. ye 3d, 1767. N.B. The ship was cast away here.' It is our earliest record of the very many wrecks which have occurred on the island.

The greatest disaster in Conwy Bay was the sinking of the paddle-steamer *Rothsay Castle* while on a day trip from Liverpool to Beaumaris on 18 August 1831. Underpowered and worn out, she had been built in 1816 for service on the Clyde. When she arrived at Liverpool for service along the Welsh coast several men refused to sail in her – one man's refusal to join her crew shortly before her last voyage was later accepted as proof of his sanity by the Manchester Commissioners in Lunacy. However the finer points of a decrepit ship such as rotting timbers, the absence of a signal gun and but one ship's boat, and that with a hole in the bottom and no oars, escaped the notice of 150 middle-class city folk who paid their money to join the *Rothsay Castle* on the morning of 17 August. Intended to sail at 10.00 am and delayed at first by the weather, and then by the late arrival of a Mr Forster, of London, who wanted his carriage hoisted aboard, the 34 nhp paddler eventually rattled her way to sea at about mid-day.

There she met the full force of a strong NNW wind and the flood tide. The ship's bandsmen, who had been playing distracting music, soon joined the passengers in crippling sea-sickness, and amid growing alarm a deputation of passengers asked one of their number, Mr William Tarrey, agent to Lord Derby, to beg the captain to put about. Mr Tarrey, who was accompanied by his 35-year-old wife Alice, and five children, was only too willing to oblige, but found Capt Atkinson drunk in his cabin, and got no more than a blasphemous refusal for his interference. It was after 5.00 pm before the captain appeared on deck and by that time the seams of the ship had begun to open and the cabin floors were awash. 'This night will tell a tale,' he prophesied. At 10.00 pm they passed the Great Orme, having taken ten hours to progress thirty-six miles. Passengers familiar with the journey knew that Beaumaris was no longer very far away, but as Puffin Island appeared on the starboard bow a fireman came on deck to say there was two feet of water in the stokehold, and the ship would soon be deprived of steam.

Passengers were ordered to man the pumps, but like everything else on the ship these proved to be useless. The men then volunteered to form a bucket chain to attempt to bail her out, but were told that the only bucket had fallen overboard. Soon afterwards the *Rothsay Castle* bumped hard on to the unseen Dutchman's Bank. Cursing the helmsman, whom he blamed for never having known how to steer, the captain gave the order 'full astern' only to be told that the fires were out. The ship then bumped for a mile or more before breaking up.

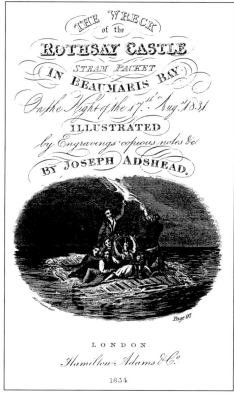

Engravings from an 1834 book telling the harrowing story of the wreck of the Rothsay Castle at the eastern mouth of the Menai Strait. One illustration depicts the successful use of women's skirts as sails with which one party of survivors reached the shore near Penmaenmawr.

First the tall iron funnel collapsed, taking the main-mast with it, smashing the side of the ship, and sweeping the captain to his death. 'I observed the vessel parting, the bow with its quivering mast leaning one way, the stern the other,' wrote one of the twenty-three survivors, a Mr Tinne, who clung to a piece of floating wreckage until rescued in the morning by a boat which put out from Beaumaris.

Nine of the survivors, including a Miss Whittaker, were saved from the drifting poop after a strange argument among the men over the propriety of asking the only lady in their company to give them her skirts for use as a sail. 'But Miss Whittaker was a lady of spirit,' said one commentator, 'and also divested herself of her garters.' Bodies were washed ashore over a considerable distance. Mrs Tarrey's grave can still be seen on the Great Orme; that of her two-year-old son John by the door of Glanconwy parish church, three miles up the river Conwy. John Thompson was buried at Formby, in Lancashire, his wife with many other victims, rests in Beaumaris churchyard. At the subsequent inquest at Beaumaris Sir Richard Williams Bulkeley, foreman of the jury, declared in a written memorandum to the coroner: 'From the evidence brought before them the jury on this inquest cannot separate without expressing their firm conviction that had the *Rothsay Castle* been a seaworthy vessel, and properly manned, this awful calamity might have been averted. They, therefore, cannot disguise their indignation at the conduct of those who could place such a vessel on this station....'

The disaster led to the establishment of Penmon lifeboat station in 1832 and the building of Penmon lighthouse, which came into use in 1837. The wreck dominated the North Wales Eisteddfod held at Beaumaris Castle in 1832, in the presence of the future Queen Victoria, and her mother, the Duchess of Kent. Nineteen entries were received for the principal competition, an ode on the subject of the wreck, and Princess Victoria was presented with a set of drawings, bound in gold-trimmed morocco, depicting the sinking.

Dutchman's Bank and Lavan Sands have claimed many vessels in what has every appearance of a broad expanse of deep water for much of each tidal cycle. There was the *Atlas*, a sloop lost in November 1832, and resulting in an RNLI medal for Griff Parry, of Penmaenmawr; there was the *Jane & Ann*, wrecked on the Lavan Sands on 20 February 1833, the *St George*, lost at the entrance to Beaumaris two days later; the *Auckland*, of Dublin, aground near Friars Road, Beaumaris, also on 22 February 1833; a schooner was wrecked on the 25th, three more vessels on the 26th; the *Britannia*, in 1837.

The *Supply*, a Pwllheli sloop of 27 tons, was lost on Puffin Island in 1838; *La Jollie Fille*, a schooner, of Caerhun, was lost by fire in Conwy Bay in 1840; the *Ellinor*, of Caernarfon, lost near Beaumaris in 1844; the *Varchwel*, a sloop of Caerhun, lost in Conwy Estuary in October 1844, when Richard Thomas, of Conwy, received a telescope from the RNLI for saving the life of John Wrench. The *Cossack* was lost in Conwy Bay in November 1845, and two tombstones at Penmon give details of five people drowned in an unnamed shipwreck on Christmas Eve 1848. The *Brothers*, a smack, of Liverpool, was wrecked at Penmon in 1850.

Eleven vessels were lost in the bay during the *Royal Charter* gale of 1859. There was the *Messenger*, of Caernarfon, wrecked near the present Beaumaris lifeboat house; the *Jane*, of Barmouth, smashed against Penmon Point; the *Alma*, a two-masted schooner, driven ashore at Penmaenmawr; the *Duchess of Gloucester*, wrecked near Llandudno Junction ferry; the *Joseph*, of Liverpool, wrecked at Deganwy; the *Handy*, abandoned at Conwy but later salvaged; the *Robert*, of Liverpool, wrecked at Conwy; the *Hectorine*, of Preston, broken up on Conwy Bar; the *Sylph*, of Newquay, Cardiganshire, foundered in Conwy harbour, the crew being saved after four hours in the rigging; the *Alice*, which sank in Conwy channel; and the *Eagles*, of Conwy, wrecked on the bar. One remarkable vessel, the 50-ton sloop *Success*, of Aberdyfi, was damaged at Conwy that October night but survived. She was built at Penhelig, Aberdyfi, in 1802 and continued sailing from Cardigan Bay until 1868, when she went to the breakers at Milford.

When the *Mary*, of Amlwch, was destroyed by fire at Conwy in March 1862 the Conwy &

Swept ashore while trying to tie up at Penmaenmawr quarry pier, on 5 November 1967, the 1,000-ton Rethi Müller, of Hamburg, had to be dug out of the sand before she could be hauled back to sea twelve days later.

The Rethi Müller *at high tide, Penmaenmawr.*

Llanrwst Railway Co lost a valuable cargo of rails for their project. It was the construction of this railway, with its raised embankment on part of the former river bed, which ended Glanconwy's days as a port and shipbuilding centre – and makes it difficult for the people of today to understand how the 45-ton Conwy sloop *Ann Margaret* could have been wrecked beneath Glanconwy rectory.

Pleasure piers have always been vulnerable and Beaumaris pier was damaged in 1868 when the 12-ton Conwy smack *Louisa Dorrock* was wrecked against it. All wooden vessels leaked somewhere and many were lost simply because the leak became more than the crew could cope with. Such was the case with the 68-ton Falmouth brigantine *Hero* which left Runcorn on 12 December 1868 with a cargo of rock salt intended for Ghent. Utterly exhausted after pumping their way across Liverpool Bay, the crew of four gave up the struggle when about two miles north of Puffin Island and took to their boat. They landed at Llaneilian next morning. The loss of the Conwy flat *Hester*, off Penmaenmawr, on 2 January 1875 reminds us of the former hectic mining activity in the Conwy Valley. She was carrying a cargo of sulphur ore intended for Runcorn and her crew of two were rescued by Llandudno lifeboat.

A tremendous gale swept across Britain during the four days 17-20 November 1893 and one of the casualties was the 1,000-ton steamship *Ivanhoe*, of Glasgow. Carrying a cargo of oranges from Liverpool to Cardiff she narrowly missed being dashed to pieces on the Great Orme and was swept into shallow water where she grounded, half-a-mile off Llandudno's West Shore. Llandudno lifeboat was launched but after a two-hour struggle was driven back to the shore. The crew then decided to try a lighter boat and borrowed the *Nightingale*, a local pleasure boat which was conveyed across the isthmus on a grocer's lorry. This time the lifeboatmen boarded the steamer and stayed with her all night, assisting to refloat her next day – 19 November – and to beach her at a safer place up river from where she was again refloated on the 21st after the gale had abated.

The Newquay, Cornwall, schooner *Lady Agnes* was wrecked in similar circumstances on 8 October 1896 during the highest tide within living memory in the bay. Built in 1877 at Trevaunance Cove, St Agnes, this fine schooner was being captained for the first time by William Cox who, with a crew of three, was taking her to Ellesmere Port. With her sails torn away when off the Great Orme during the previous evening, the *Lady Agnes* lit distress torches at quarter-hour intervals throughout the night, but her signals were not seen until daybreak. All attempts to launch the lifeboat at the West Shore failed and the schooner was driven on to the rocks near the remains of the Bishop's Palace. As their vessel proceeded to break up the crew succeeded in floating spars ashore to establish a rope link with which they were all saved.

The last schooner to be wrecked on this unpredictable shore was the 200-ton *Flying Foam*, of Bridgewater, whose keel may still be seen at low tide but a short distance from the West Shore car park. Built at Jersey in 1879, she was never fitted with auxiliary power and was still a pure sailing vessel when she anchored between Puffin Island and Penmaenmawr to repair a sail on 21 January 1936. Caught by a worsening wind, she dragged her anchor to drift ashore with a heavy cargo of coal. Beaumaris lifeboat took off the crew of six and several Conwy trawlermen later boarded the schooner to try to keep her pumped out, but she began to break up and had to be abandoned. The wreck was sold to a Llandudno coal merchant.

Damaged by enemy action, the MV *Gleneden* entered Conwy Bay on 28 January 1940, possibly looking for a suitable beaching site. She grounded on the north-west corner of Dutchman's Bank, about a quarter of a mile from Puffin Island, but the incoming tide washed the sand from under her and she began to break up. Moelfre lifeboat took off her crew of sixty in two trips. Holed on a rock near Puffin Island, HMS *St Olaves*, a 468-ton tug, was abandoned by her crew of thirty-one on 13 April 1941. Finding the crew already in their boats, Beaumaris lifeboat decided to try to save the tug and some of the naval men reboarded her for a tow.

The decks were awash when the tug was abandoned for the second time off Friars mudflats. Subsequently repaired and refloated, the *St Olaves* was finally wrecked off Dunscansby Head on 21 September 1942.

In September 1940 the Coast Artillery School was moved from its traditional home at Shoeburyness, Essex, to Llandudno, part of it to massive gun emplacements beneath the Great Orme and part in the shadow of the Little Orme. With an instructional capacity of 150 officers, 115 officer cadets and 445 other ranks it was responsible for the firing of an enormous number of shells during the course of the war and one too accurate salvo accidentally sank the 5,300-ton target ship *Ghambira,* four miles NNE of Puffin Island on 15 October 1943. The wreck was further reduced by explosive charges after the war.

The MV *River Loyne* vanished after leaving Penmaenmawr quarry pier with a load of stone on 7 December 1948. Some days later a ship's lamp was found in a trawler's net and then a mast was spotted sticking out of the sea a mile SE by S of the northern tip of Puffin Island. Her crew were never found.

When the 1,000-ton German ship *Rethi Müller* was driven ashore at Penmaenmawr, on 5 November 1967, the 152-year-old Llandudno LSA team made their first recorded breeches buoy rescue – of a Llandudno woman. The largest ship ever to tie up at the end of the 614ft-long quarry pier, the *Rethi Müller* was still empty when caught by a 50 mph wind early on that Sunday morning. At 10.00 am Captain Franz Hintz reported that despite extra mooring ropes, the pier would not hold him and soon afterwards the 235ft-long vessel swung broadside on to the sea. The snapping of the last of the lines ensnared the 68-year-old bo'sun, Hans Lucht, who broke a leg and was taken off at the height of the storm by an RAF helicopter. As the ship continued to drag her anchor towards a lee shore coastguard Divisional Officer Fred Bushel, of Holyhead, instructed the Llandudno LSA team, led by Mr Eric Williams, to put a rocket line aboard. However the German crew decided to stay with their ship, although they put their woman guest ashore.

The drama was played out in full view of much of Penmaenmawr and those who could not watch from their windows gathered on the shingle beach where the *Rethi Müller* was eventually cast ashore. Owned by Otto A. Müller, of Hamburg, she was a sister ship to the *Birgit Müller,* a frequent caller at Penmaenmawr, which only eleven days earlier had sunk in three minutes after a collision with the Greek ship *Anghyra,* in the Thames.

Salvage of the *Rethi Müller* was entrusted to Ulrich Harms, of Hamburg, who, with Risdon Beazley, of Southampton, formed the consortium which rescued the SS *Great Britain* from the Falkland Islands in 1970. Bulldozers were used to excavate a deep channel to the sea while the hull was raised off the shingle with plastic rollers which were inflated with compressed air. By using bulldozers as rams the ship was refloated into the artificial channel late on 17 November, turned stern-on to the sea on the morning tide of the 18th and hauled clear by tugs on the afternoon tide.

Among those who watched the thirteen days of round-the-clock activity from his home was Mr Ivor E. Davies, the Penmaenmawr historian, who recalled earlier incidents involving quarry boats. In the 1930s the *Jolly Charles,* a three-masted steamer of about 600-tons, was already partly loaded when blown ashore on the Conwy side of the pier. To facilitate her discharge a 3ft-gauge railway was laid across the promenade and down the beach. With the aid of a shuttle service of tubs, borrowed from the quarry railway, several hundred tons of granite chippings were removed and dumped on the promenade where they were presented to Penmaenmawr Urban Council as an unexpected windfall, and used for many a year for roadworks in the town. Most of the mishaps involved vessels tied up at what used to be a second quarry pier half-a-mile to the west of the one still standing. The *Emerald,* a ship which went adrift in the early 1930s, was remembered because a sailor lost his life while trying to leap to the safety of the pier.

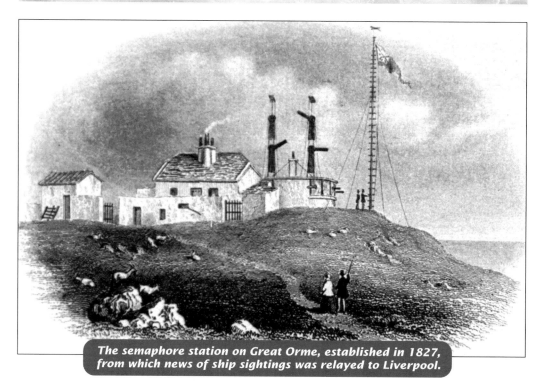

The semaphore station on Great Orme, established in 1827, from which news of ship sightings was relayed to Liverpool.

Part of the keel of the Flying Foam *appears periodically out of the beach exposed at low tide below the West Shore car park, at Llandudno. Built in 1879, she was swept ashore with a cargo of coal on 21 January 1936.*

Conwy trawlermen are acknowledged experts on the navigation of the North Wales coast and when they are involved in any mishap it is usually in the role of rescuers. However, on 22 April 1969 the *Glenmaye* was wrecked on Puffin Island. Although registered at Liverpool she had worked from Conwy since 1950, being owned by Archie Barr, who was also her skipper. With the *Glenmore* (skipper Peter Barr), and *Glendale* (skipper Ken Barr), the *Glenmaye* was making for the shelter of the Menai Strait. She was the last of the three as they ran from worsening weather in Llandudno Bay, and struck a submerged rock off the uninhabited island. 'At the time the crew were on deck gutting fish and moments before we struck I had been speaking to one of them,' said Mr Barr. 'It was raining and misty and we were being lashed by heavy seas,' he said, adding:

> The moment we struck the boat was driven broadside on, and seas swept over her. I realised immediately that she was badly damaged and I shouted to the crew to jump. I put out a radio call asking if anyone was around to help us but before I got a reply the wheelhouse was flooded and the radio went dead. The crew put on lifejackets and jumped into the sea. After they had left the boat I managed to grab some distress flares and threw them to the men.

He joined the men in the water and they all managed to scramble up the cliffs of Puffin Island to a ledge 100ft above the sea from where they fired their flares. Two tugs sheltering off Anglesey saw their signals and Beaumaris lifeboat and an RAF helicopter were turned out. 'The lifeboat offered to send over a breeches buoy but I refused as we were all safe on the ledge and someone might have got hurt,' said Mr Barr. Meanwhile the *Glenmore* and *Glendale* had returned to the opposite side of the island, where they were sheltered from the worst of the storm, and the two skippers along with three of their men went ashore on a self-inflating liferaft. They crossed the island and, while one of the tugs pinpointed the marooned men with a searchlight, ropes were lowered for a rescue up the sheer cliff face.

Lord Langford, Lord of the Manor of Rhuddlan and Constable of Rhuddlan Castle, was stranded on Puffin Island with a party of friends when his cabin cruiser *Wendy Sue* sank on 19 August 1970. Two crewmen who took to the dinghy were picked up by the *Ripper Venturer,* a local fishing-boat which raised the alarm. The party on the island were rescued by Beaumaris lifeboat and the *Wendy Sue* was raised by a trawler two days later – minus two picnic hampers and three anoraks. 'Everything else was intact even a bottle of whisky. It was amazing considering the boat was hauled back under water for eight miles,' said Lord Langford. The former library of Lord Langford's ancestral home at Bodrhyddan Hall, Rhuddlan, is decorated with some intriguing sixteenth-century wall panels. They combine religious carvings with Dutch inscriptions and, according to family tradition, the panels once formed the chapel reredos aboard a Spanish Armada ship wrecked on the coast of North Wales.

The most recent wreck buoy to be placed in position on this coast marks the *Hoveringham II,* a 480-ton sand dredger which sank 350 yd off shore, near Penmon quarry jetty, on 28 January 1971. Her upturned hull is clearly visible at low water. She sprang a leak in Puffin Sound, while on passage from Liverpool for Port Penrhyn, and four of her crew were taken off by Beaumaris lifeboat. The remaining three left later as the dredger began to capsize.

Exactly a year later, on 28 January 1972, the 499-ton Hamburg coaster *Hohenlinden,* approaching Penmaenmawr at night, ran aground close to the quarry pier. She was refloated on the rising tide and, after collecting a 873-ton cargo of granite chippings, sailed only to be sunk within forty-eight hours. She went down rapidly after being involved in a collision in the North Sea on 31 January. One of her crew of eight and a woman passenger were drowned.

No ship tied up at Penmaenmawr pier after 1976, the year in which 54-year-old submarine hero Lieutenant-Commander Neil Rutherford, DSC and Bar, former commanding officer of HMS *Spiteful,* went berserk at the nearby Red Gables Hotel – built in 1885 by the quarry housing contractor. He shot and killed his four fellow occupants and then shot himself, with the German pistol he had brought home from the war.

The troublesome greenheart pier, by then 96 years old, was demolished in 1984, after Kingston Minerals had opened a new rail head and computer controlled conveyor from their granite crushers.

WHEN viewed from the sea, the Great Orme looms up like an enormous dragon's head to which the setting sun adds the illusion of flaming mouth and nostrils; hence its name from the Viking *ormr,* meaning 'serpent'. It is a limestone mass which juts two miles into the sea, is a mile wide and rises by sheer cliffs to a height of 679ft. Awesome enough on a fine day (although frequently used as a shelter from westerly storms) it was a dreaded obstacle to navigation in the days of sail. Its first known victim was the *Phoenix,* a vessel hired at Dublin in the autumn of 1641 to reinforce HMS *Swan* and the armed pinnace *Confidence* for action against the Catholic uprising in Ulster. Commanded by Capt John Bartlett, soon to earn fame as admiral of the king's fleet in the Irish Sea during the English Civil War, the *Swan* was a ship of about 200 tons. The *Confidence* was of 100 tons with ten guns and a crew of forty, a description which probably also applied to the *Phoenix.* Just why an Irish privateer engaged in the suppression of an Irish Catholic rebellion should have been 'cast away at Orme's Head in Caernarvonshire' in January 1642 remains a mystery which the records do not explain. Nor is there any reference to survivors, although the vessel was not a total loss for her guns were salvaged and conveyed to Chester in February to be loaded aboard the *Swan.*

Hornby Cave, at the westernmost point of the Great Orme, commemorates the loss of the 280-ton Liverpool brig *Hornby* late on New Year's Day 1824. With a crew of thirteen, two passengers and a cargo valued at £60,000, the brig had left for Rio de Janeiro on 27 December. Her master was a man named Wade, formerly a lieutenant in command of the revenue cutter *Defence* stationed in Conwy Bay. 'His family resided at Beaumaris and rumour described him as a very cross-grained, disagreeable man and not popular in the town,' wrote Thomas Peers Williams, MP, of Craig-y-don, near Menai Bridge, in a letter to Sir Llewelyn Turner, of Caernarvon. He continued:

> However, be that as it may, when the cutter was paid off he went to reside in Liverpool and got the command of a trader called the *Hornby,* and sailed with a valuable general cargo; but having got as far as Point Lynas he met with bad weather and a north-west wind which prevented his making Holyhead, and was two days struggling between Orme's Head and Lynas. On the second night, however, between four and five bells of the middle watch, the mate ineffectually endeavoured to persuade his commander to go into Beaumaris, but he said: 'I had rather be at sea for ever than go there.' Thinking it was time to go about, he sent a man to loose the jib, but the man had no sooner got on the jib-boom than seeing a rock just below him, he jumped upon it. When he recovered himself he saw no more of the ship and, the next morning, he clambered up the precipice and told the story. There were afterwards nineteen (sic) people sent to Caernarvon gaol for plundering the wreck. (Actual figures were ten convictions and three acquittals.)

John Williams, the man who jumped from the jib-boom was the only survivor. He related his escape to a group of disbelieving copper miners whom he found assembled around the

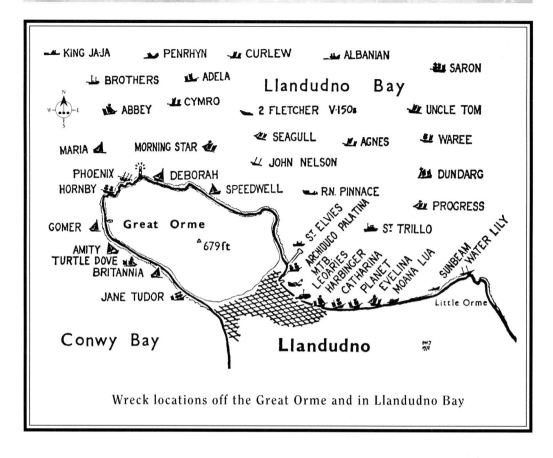

Wreck locations off the Great Orme and in Llandudno Bay

Llandudno smithy. Williams spent the rest of his working life as a miner and in old age lived off the coins of tourists who were delighted to hear the tale of a genuine shipwrecked mariner. As late as 1877 the Llandudno pleasure-boat owners were claiming to be able to show visitors parts of the wreckage of the *Hornby*.

In 1836 a Parliamentary Select Committee appointed to investigate the inadequacy of harbour facilities on the north-eastern coast of England were asked to extend their examination to North Wales, with particular reference to the Great Orme. They reported:

> It appears to your Committee that on the north-west coast of Wales there is a great deficiency of harbours of refuge for ships sailing to and from Liverpool; that great facilities are offered for such a harbour between the Great and Little Orme's Heads, which would prevent very great losses as appears by a return extracted from Lloyd's books, and would be a good station for pilots required for taking vessels into the Mersey.

Simultaneously a Select Committee on Shipwrecks was sitting and they reported:

> In the present year, 1836, no less than thirty-nine vessels were seen on shore at Holyhead Bay at one time, twenty of which were totally lost; and within the same period many vessels have been wrecked between Holyhead and Liverpool, where an excellent position exists for forming a harbour of refuge between the Great and Little Orme's Heads, at which, had such a harbour been formed, the greater number of these vessels might have been saved.

Before the year was out the St George's Harbour & Railway Co issued a prospectus for the construction of a railway from Chester to Llandudno, where they proposed to build a new harbour to replace Holyhead as the Irish packet station. In 1837 the Irish Railway Commission surveyed an alternative route from Shrewsbury to Porthdinllaen (see Chapter Three), while in 1838 the Chester & Crewe Railway Co engaged George Stephenson to survey the route from Chester to Holyhead. By 1844 George Stephenson's equally renowned son, Robert, had still not come up with his eventual solution for bridging the Menai Strait and on 26 February of that year yet another competitior, the North Wales & Dublin Railway & Harbour Co, revived the original Llandudno plan. In a lengthy memorandum to the Lords Commissioners of the Treasury they summarised the problems of sailing from the Mersey:

> With a strong southerly wind vessels do not hesitate to proceed to sea from Liverpool; by the time they reach the Skerries they almost invariably find it south-west; by keeping under the land they easily get down off Point Lynas, where it not infrequently comes on to blow a gale from the westward; if it increases they cannot beat to windward round the Skerries and have no alternative (there being no shelter on their lee, or along the whole coast) but to turn back towards Liverpool, with the risk of being driven on the sands; whereas if there were a refuge harbour at the Orme's Heads the commanders of vessels would keep at sea another night, knowing that at the last extremity there was shelter at hand; and when a vessel can round the Skerries she can go to sea and therefore stands in no need of shelter at Holyhead. It is not an uncommon circumstance for 150 sail to put to sea in one tide from Liverpool, and to be driven back by contrary winds before they can reach the Skerries.

Their scheme would have created a 90-acre harbour linked to a railway terminus on the site of the present Grand Hotel, Llandudno. A sea wall would have extended for 720yd in the direction of the Little Orme and then would have turned due south for 370yd. As a second phase they suggested extending the sea wall to enclose the whole of the 800-acre bay.

Such a harbour would undoubtedly have prevented many a shipwreck, although it would not have saved the 345-ton American barque *Jane Tudor* which struck the Great Orme while on her maiden voyage on 15 February 1847. Brief details were recorded in his visitors' book by Bernard Watson, keeper of the semaphore telegraph station on the site of the present Summit Hotel:

> The barque *Jane Tudor,* of Bath, Maine, on her passage from Baltimore, towards Liverpool, laden with corn and flour, was wrecked in Hell's Mouth on the west side of Greatormeshead. Commander, Nathan T. Thompson, of Bowden, Maine; Chief Mate, James P. Alexander, of Richmond, Maine; Second Mate, Stephen Stuart, of Richmond.

The wreck with contents was auctioned at the Castle Hotel, Conwy, and knocked down to a Liverpool man for £210, the sails being sold separately for £45. On the following day the successful bidder sold the *Jane Tudor,* in situ, to two Conwy men, Richard Thomas, who owned a local shipyard, and Thomas Jones, a timber merchant. With the aid of two Liverpool tugs they refloated their purchase on a very high tide and took her into Conwy where she was repaired and put back into service with a Beaumaris registration. She sailed for many a year between Conwy and Montreal and it was claimed that no vessel carried as much timber as the *Jane Tudor* for the construction of modern Llandudno during the boom years 1850-70.

Another wreck of 1847 has been carved upon the Llandudno folk-memory as 'the Indian corn ship.' She was an Italian two-masted brig named the *Archiduco Palatino* which was driven against a cliff then known as Clawdd-y-Gorad on the site of the present Grand Hotel. With her sails torn, she had been tossed about the bay for an hour before she struck at about

Crippled by the rocks beneath the western cliffs of the Great Orme and still flying a distress signal after being swept across Conwy Bay in 1870, the Caernarfon schooner Turtle Dove became a total loss on the next tide.

eleven o'clock in the morning. Scores of people watched the inevitable, among them the sons of Sam Brookes, of the Victoria Inn, who had just bought a new boat called the *Lady Harriet*. As soon as the brig grounded the local boat was launched but after a struggle lasting several minutes the *Lady Harriet* was overturned and swept ashore, together with her exhausted crew. Eight of the eleven men aboard the *Archiduco Palatino* then put to sea in their own boat but this, too, was overturned and sank with the loss of three lives. The remaining five were rescued, as were the three who remained on the brig until the tide had receded.

The cargo proved too much of a temptation for the people of Llandudno and led to what is still known as *Y Diarddel Mawr*, 'the Big Excommunication'. The trouble began one Sunday morning when customs officers from Conwy met a horse and cart laden with Indian corn making its way out of Llandudno along Llanrhos road. They turned back the offending farmer and made him dump his stolen load near the present war memorial. Before long the officers had recovered a huge mound of corn and special chapel meetings were held to discuss the scandal. Zealous circuit superintendents expelled all the Llandudno Wesleyan Methodists, all but two Presbyterians and all but three of the Baptists for doing what they had always done whenever the good Lord had delivered a strange ship into their hands.

The Inspector of Lifeboats visited Llandudno early in 1860 and recommended that a boat should be stationed at the young resort. The RNLI accepted his report at their August meeting and in the following month two sisters, the Misses Brown, of Toxteth Park, Liverpool, made a donation of £200, in memory of a third sister, and stipulated that the money should be used to supply a lifeboat to Llandudno where all three had spent some happy holidays. They also asked for the boat to be named the *Sisters' Memorial,* this being the first occasion in the history of the RNLI for a boat to be named by its donors.

Sisters' Memorial was delivered by rail on 18 January 1861 and the first call for her services came on 9 February when Job Jones, keeper of the telegraph station, received a semaphore message from Point of Ayr stating that a schooner was in distress and drifting towards Llandudno. Before the lifeboat could be launched a second message was received stating that the unidentified schooner had sunk near Rhyl. Llandudno lifeboat crew were similarly thwarted on the following day when Penmon lifeboat beat them to the Fleetwood schooner *Village Maid,* aground on the Dutchman's Bank in Conwy Bay. The first rescue from Llandudno was on Friday 13 September 1861 when the crew of three were taken off the Runcorn flat *Uncle Tom,* which was seen flying a distress signal as it slowly sank with its cargo of coal intended for Caernarvon. The last rescue by the *Sisters' Memorial* was on 7 December 1866 when two men were taken off the smack *Cymro.* In the following February the lifeboat failed to reach an unidentified vessel in distress north of the town and was herself driven before the wind to capsize when about a mile off Rhyl. All the lifeboatmen survived the incident but an official inquiry upheld the view of the coxswain that the boat was particularly prone to being swamped and she was replaced by *Sisters' Memorial II.*

Llandudno shipwrecks of the next two decades included: *Jane,* a Caernarfon smack abandoned six miles north of the town in 1867, but later taken in tow by the SS *Prince Arthur; Brothers,* of Beaumaris, 1867; *Catharina, a* 100-ton Dutch brigantine, 1869; *Gomer,* a sloop, of Nefyn, 1870; *Maria,* a Pwllheli sloop, 1870; *Turtle Dove,* a Caernarfon schooner, 1870; *Speedwell,* a Pwllheli sloop, 1876; SS *Albanian,* of the Bibby Line, sunk by collision off the Great Orme 1877; SS *King Ja-Ja,* of the Liverpool, Caernarvon & Menai Straits Steamship Co, abandoned by her crew of ten but reboarded, 1877; *Water Lilly,* 1887; and *Heide,* a Liverpool cutter, 1887. Newspaper reports of the bravery of the Llandudno lifeboatmen helped them to top the poll, with Brighton second, in a national competition run by the makers of 'Sunlight' soap to find the two stations most worthy of new lifeboats. The result was the arrival in October 1887 of the ill-fated *Sunlight No 1.* She alerted the superstitious during her naming launch when Second Coxswain Edward Jones took ill, to die

The Schooner Flying Foam
on Llandudno beach.

The Schooner Flying Foam
sinking off Llandudno West
shore in June, 1936.

a few days later from what was described as 'a chill'. This was regarded as a bad omen and the sad day came when the crew of *Sunlight No 1* mutinied, a shore helper was killed, the coxswain was dismissed and the lifeboat secretary resigned. The unhappy train of events began when John Austin, keeper of the Great Orme lighthouse, ran into town during the great gale which swept Britain on 7 November 1890. He reported that the Caernarfon brigantine *Planet*, laden with coal, was being swept to destruction and he himself went out with the lifeboat to help in the rescue of the crew of five. Later in the same morning a Norwegian barque, the *Saron*, was sighted in distress about seven miles NNE of the lighthouse. The lifeboat crew were assembled but refused to put to sea, alleging that Coxswain Richard Jones was drunk. Dr Dalton, a local practitioner, climbed on to the launching carriage and appealed for volunteers, at the same time ordering Richard Jones out of the boat. While helping to manhandle the boat across the beach a man named Robert Williams slipped beneath the carriage and was killed. The lifeboat was at sea for several hours but found nothing, the barque having been taken in tow by a passing tug. Two years later *Sunlight No 1* claimed her third victim when a man named Arthur Whalley fell beneath the launching carriage.

Four vessels were wrecked in Llandudno Bay on 1 February 1892. Several had been sheltering from a worsening westerly gale and the first to put up distress signals was the Beaumaris schooner *Abbey*. The lifeboat was prevented from going to her assistance when an axle of the launching carriage broke on the beach but the piermaster and four volunteers put to sea in a small rowing boat and rescued the crew. A similar rescue was made later in the day when seven men took out the pleasure boat *Nightingale* to rescue the one man aboard the flat *Agnes*, which foundered in the bay. Two Beaumaris vessels, the *Seagull* and the *John Nelson*, signalled for help in the afternoon but by this time the lifeboat was able to launch and a total of five men were rescued – the lifeboat returning just in time to be relaunched for the quarterly practice!

The Nefyn barque *Eivion* flew distress signals off the Great Orme in December 1893 but with assistance from the lifeboat survived, to be wrecked off South America in 1904. The *Waree*, a brigantine, foundered in the bay in 1896; the *Curlew*, of Conwy, sank some eight miles north of the Great Orme in 1898; and the last wreck of the century was the *Harbinger*, a schooner laden with coal for Ireland, which quickly broke up after being driven ashore opposite Craig-y-don Parade on 10 November 1899.

Regattas have been a feature of Llandudno since at least 1860 but it was thirty-five years later before the first steps were taken to form a sailing club. By 1896 the club's sprit-sail half-raters were prominent on the north-western yachting scene – and by the evening of 3 August 1900 most of them were at the bottom of the sea after one of the worst storms in the town's history. It was the Friday of the August bank holiday weekend and the big keel-boats were anchored in the bay after the fashion adopted for very many years by the local boatmen who plied for hire, did some fishing and put down lobster pots. 'Several of the local sailing boats were swamped whilst others broke loose from their anchors and were smashed to pieces,' stated the *Llandudno Advertiser,* while in the annual report of the sailing club it was recorded that: 'Our own losses were very considerable and totally irrecoverable.'

On the following Tuesday morning the Runcorn schooner *Evelina*, bound from Widnes for Port Dinorwig with a cargo of coal, lost both her main gaff and mizzen sails in Liverpool Bay and was swept uncontrollably around the Little Orme where she struck a rock. She sank opposite St Paul's church, the crew of three later being rescued from the rigging which remained visible above the sea. In the afternoon the PS *St Elvies* collided with the *St Tudno* at the pier head but was able to limp back to Liverpool for major repairs, the *St Tudno* escaping serious damage.

The most famous wreck of this Llandudno storm, 'unparalleled in the month of August,' never really happened. It was that of the 'Norwegian barque *Hjalmar*' which limped into the

The cabin cruisers Melwood and Gannet, being swept ashore at Llandudno on 3 May 1974

bay eleven years later in the pages of Arnold Bennett's delightful novel *The Card*. Never more than a creation of Bennett's fertile imagination, the 'wreck of the *Hjalmar*' was given renewed credibility in 1951 when Sir Alec Guinness, Glynis Johns, Valerie Hobson and Petula Clark turned up at Llandudno to make a highly successful film of the story.

Farce attended a naval visit to Llandudno, on 13 September 1919, when HMS *Queen Elizabeth*, HMS *Lion* and HMS *Venomous* anchored in the bay as part of a grand victory cruise. The battleships made an impressive sight off the Great Orme and North Wales was present in force to see the humiliation of Admiral Sir Charles Madden, commander-in-chief of the Atlantic Fleet, and Rear-Admiral Sir Roger Keyes, commander at the Zeebrugge and Ostend raids. The two admirals had come ashore to pay their respects at the Town Hall and to invite a party of civic dignitaries to join them for lunch on board the *Queen Elizabeth*. With careful timing the returning top brass, walking along the pier, and the admiral's steam pinnace crossing the bay, should have met at the pier head. As it was, the pinnace, running a few seconds late, came in too fast and rammed the pier steps. The hapless lieutenant in command turned about, presumably in an attempt to return to his parent ship but the damaged pinnace sank between the pier head and Pen Trwyn, its crew being rescued by the paddle-steamer *St Trillo*. After an exchange of semaphore signals another pinnace was sent out, only to repeat the performance of the first, although in this instance the coxswain had the wisdom to run his boat ashore. Before the day was finished a total of four naval steam pinnaces had been sunk at Llandudno and Admiral Madden let it be known that he had banned all future visits by the Royal Navy until the pier head had been rendered safe.

Llandudno never does anything by halves and thirty minutes after thirty-four of Britain's fastest power boats roared out of the bay, on 11 July 1965, for what was to have been a 100-mile race, three lifeboats, a helicopter and a Liverpool pilot-boat were all engaged in a major

The Anna Olga stranded on Llandudno's gently-sloping beach after becoming embayed on a lee shore

search and rescue operation. Llandudno lifeboat was joined by lifeboats from Rhyl and Beaumaris when it was reported that three of the power boats had been sunk and another eleven were unaccounted for. The final score was six boats swamped and abandoned although four were subsequently recovered, two of them by Liverpool trawlers which towed their prizes to the pier where the crews haggled for salvage money. The two boats which were lost, about four miles north of the town, were 'Fletcher' V.150 types, one of which was being driven by Mr Norman Fletcher himself.

A dramatic incident which came within an ace of a major disaster was played out in Llandudno Bay on 6 May 1968. Nearing the end of her annual 'spring adventure cruise' out of New York, the 26,677-ton Swedish American luxury liner *Kungsholm* anchored in the early morning about 1½ miles offshore. She used the 314-ton MV *St Trillo* as a tender to disembark most of her passengers for a coach trip to the mountains of Snowdonia. Weather conditions deteriorated during the afternoon and there was a 35 mph westerly wind and heavy off-shore swell by early evening when the *St Trillo* left Llandudno pier with 325 of the *Kungsholm's* American passengers, several Swedish crew members and about fifty local people who had paid 25p each for a quick sight-seeing trip around the outside of the liner and back.

As she endeavoured to tie up beside the liner the *St Trillo* fouled her port propeller on one of the mooring ropes and drifted away with a troublesome starboard engine which broke down a few minutes later. Llandudno lifeboat, the *Lilly Wainwright*, was already at sea, rounding the Great Orme after towing the Wallasey cabin-cruiser *Calypso* to Conwy. Coxswain Gordon Bellamy was asked by radio to start disembarking the passengers from the *St Trillo* and did, in fact, manage to tie up alongside. However, as most of the passengers were elderly he thought it would be unwise to ask them to jump into the badly rolling lifeboat, and Llandudno and Rhyl LSA teams were asked to stand by for a breeches-buoy rescue in the event of the *St Trillo* striking the Little Orme. Rhyl lifeboat *Anthony Robert Marshall* was launched at 7.50 pm, followed by the Beaumaris lifeboat *Field Marshal & Mrs Smuts* at 8.00 pm. As the storm worsened the *Kungsholm* weighed anchor at 8.20pm and sailed for a new position 5 miles north of Llandudno, near the West Constable Buoy. By this time most of the 420 people on board the *St Trillo* were violently sick and the surgeon of the *Kungsholm*, who happened to be on the tender, appealed for medical supplies, including insulin for several diabetics who were in distress. Llandudno lifeboat chased the *Kungsholm* to pick up a medical pack and Dr Ian Wynne Hughes, of Llandudno, went out with Rhyl lifeboat to offer his assistance to the *St Trillo*.

Meanwhile Jack Williams, skipper of the 49-ton Conwy trawler *Kilravock,* unloading at Conwy quay, happened to switch on his radio and hear an exchange of messages suggesting there was every risk of a major disaster in Llandudno Bay. Unloading was suspended and the *Kilravock* turned about just in time to clear the bar on the receding tide and head out to sea to round the Great Orme. At 10.15 pm Skipper Williams got a tow line aboard the *St Trillo* and, with superb seamanship, the helpless motor vessel was put alongside the pierhead thirty minutes later to end a six-hour ordeal for her passengers, three of whom were admitted to Llandudno Hospital.

The rescue had an ironic sequel when the *Kungsholm* next visited Llandudno on 17 May 1969 and, by way of an expression of gratitude for the previous year's efforts, a number of local people, including the skipper of the *Kilravock*, were entertained on board. During dinner the weather deteriorated so rapidly that, finding himself close to a lee shore, the captain of the *Kungsholm* decided to weigh anchor and sail north. At ten o'clock next morning his guests, unshaven and dinner-jacketed, were disembarked at Douglas, Isle of Man and flown to Liverpool, from where they returned to Llandudno by coach to complete a 220-mile substitute for what should have been a ten-minute trip in a tender.

Llandudno lighthouse, where the lantern first shone on 1 December 1862, was switched off on 22 March 1985, rendered obsolete by radar. It was built on the cliffs of the Great Orme by the Mersey Docks and Harbour Board, and taken over by Trinity House in 1973. Its light was 325ft above high water spring tides, and shone white from 099-243 degrees, with a sinister red sector up to 251 degrees. Before the lighthouse was sold, for conversion into a private house, the original lantern was removed to decorate the entrance hall of the Liverpool offices of the Mersey Docks and Harbour Company. It has since been returned to Llandudno for display at the summit of the Great Orme.

LIVERPOOL BAY

AMONG the memorials at the port of Liverpool there is a statue of Columbus inscribed: 'The discoverer of America was the maker of Liverpool.' Thirty-five miles to the west, in the shadow of the Little Orme, there is an inland remnant of an ancient quay wall bearing the interesting challenge: 'Prince Madoc sailed from here, Aber-Kerrick-Gwynan, 1170 AD and landed at Mobile, Alabama, with his ships *Gorn Gwynant* and *Pedr Sant.*' Between the two lies a sea area which was known as Chester Bar until the Dee ports surrendered to the commercial supremacy of the Mersey, since when it has been known the world over as Liverpool Bay, although the Admiralty hydrographers restrict the title to the immediate Mersey approaches on the Cheshire side of the ancient Dee boundary between England and Wales.

While creating wonderful Welsh beaches for English holiday-makers the shifting sands of Liverpool Bay have closed harbour after harbour, to the confusion of generations of mariners. Aber Cerrig Gwynion was in use until 1687, reputedly for vessels of up to thirty tons burden. The next navigable creek along the bay was the River Clwyd, diverted by Edward I during 1277-80 in conjunction with the building of his castle and naval dock at Rhuddlan, two miles from the sea. It has been calculated that the dock, which became the headquarters of the English navy during the conquest of Wales in 1282, was designed for vessels of about forty tons. Rhuddlan town quay, some 350yd downstream from the castle, was said to be in regular use by vessels of fifty tons at the time when the river was spanned by the Chester & Holyhead Railway in 1848. Today, the navigable part of the Clwyd is limited to Foryd harbour, Rhyl, which is still used by an occasional timber ship and many small pleasure boats.

The disused lighthouse at Point of Ayr, eight miles east of the Foryd, was built under a 1776 Act of Parliament for improving the navigation of the Port of Chester – a responsibility vested in the River Dee Co since 1741. The lighthouse marks the Welsh corner of the Dee estuary which is five miles wide, except for Hilbre Island a mile off the Cheshire shore. The presence of the West Hoyle Bank, across the mouth of the estuary, has made navigation of the Dee a somewhat hazardous operation for several centuries but this did not prevent extensive harbour development on both banks between the sea and Chester, which is twenty-one miles inland from Point of Ayr. Natural siltation and land reclamation schemes make it difficult to recognise some of the Deeside towns as former ports and there is now a new road crossing near the mouth of the estuary.

'The constant alterations in the Hoyle and Burbo sand banks are well known, for where the best channel is one week, in another it becomes a sand bank,' wrote the chart maker William Morris, in 1801, when describing the approach to Liverpool. He added:

> None but good pilots, who are here as capable as any in Great Britain, and who are in constant practice in and out of the harbour, and who are always examining the depth of water and taking new leading marks as the alteration of the sands may require, can pretend to carry a ship in or out of port with any chance of safety.

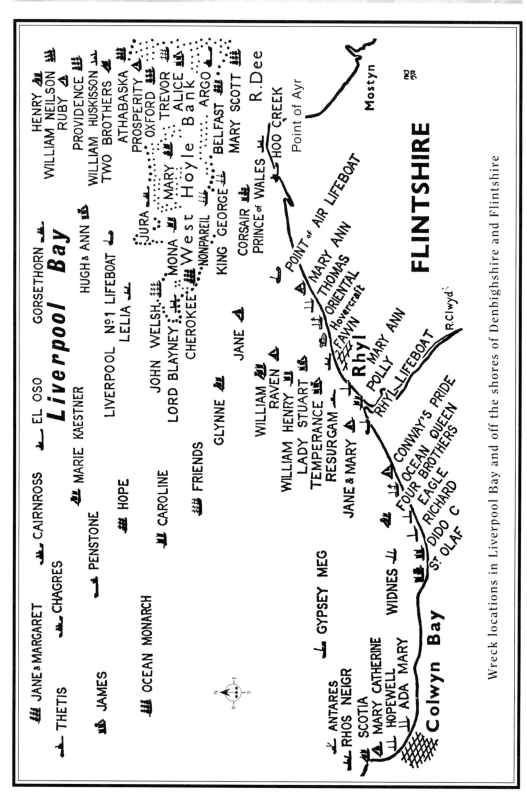

Wreck locations in Liverpool Bay and off the shores of Denbighshire and Flintshire

Britain's first submarine, the Resurgam, lies in shallow water off Rhyl, where she disappeared during her trials in 1880.

Ironically, our first recorded shipwreck on the Hoyle Bank was the pilot cutter *Two Brothers* in November 1770. It was named after the Liverpool brothers William and John Bibby, the latter being drowned in the mishap. Two Irish Sea packets, the *Nonpareil* and *Trevor,* were lost on the Hoyle on 19 October 1775. There was one survivor out of forty-seven on board when the *Betty & Mary,* of Newry, struck the Hoyle on 18 March 1791; only the captain was saved when the Caernarfon brigantine *Mary* sprang a leak on the Hoyle on 26 April 1792; and all were lost when the *Lovely Peggy,* of Red Wharf Bay, sank between the West Hoyle and East Hoyle on 20 March 1793. The *Hope* and the *Belfast* vanished when an unexpected storm blew up soon after they left the Mersey on 12 November 1799. Some 300 emigrants for America, many of them from South Caernarvonshire, were on board an unnamed ship which was holed on a rock near the Skerries early in April 1801. Contact was made with a Liverpool-bound brig which took off the women and children but the men were left behind to man the pumps. The ship drifted across Liverpool Bay and the captain, who had earlier declared 'We are all lost,' was drunk and incapable when his seamanship was required for entering the channel. The vessel struck the Hoyle Bank in the early hours of the morning, although everyone appears to have been rescued on the following day. Passengers aboard the Irish packet *King George* were less fortunate in similar circumstances in August 1806 when 106 lives were lost on the Hoyle.

Wesleyan Methodism suffered a major setback with the earliest-known wreck at the opposite end of the bay. This was the 43-ton Caernarfon sloop *Mary Catherine* which was driven ashore on 18 January 1820 at Llandrillo-yn-rhos, now usually known as Rhos-on-Sea. Precise details have been lost but the congregation at Bron-y-nant chapel, a mile inland, were disciplined for robbing the wreck. Unlike the Llandudno Nonconformists who were expelled in similar circumstances in 1847 (see Chapter Nine), the congregation at Bron-y-nant rejected the judgement of their circuit superintendent and divorced themselves from orthodox Methodism. They closed their doors to circuit ministers for nearly seven years but continued to meet as an independent church.

Relentlessly the Hoyle Bank exacted its toll. Eighty lives were lost when the Dublin packet *Earl of Moira* struck the bank on 15 August 1821; all on board were lost when the *William Neilson* foundered in the Mersey approaches on 8 October 1832; again all were lost when the SS *Lord Blayney,* bound from Newry to Liverpool with a cargo of livestock and butter, struck the West Hoyle on 11 December 1833; thirteen of the fifteen on board, including the pilot, were drowned when the *John Welsh* of Savanilla, hit the West Hoyle on 29 July 1836. Very often the victims were emigrants. The *Jane & Margaret* met with some unknown disaster after leaving Liverpool on 6 February 1837 with 200 cabin passengers for New York: part of her wreckage and two bodies were washed ashore on the Isle of Man. The full-rigged British ship *Athabaska* was lost on the West Hoyle on 17 April 1838 after leaving Liverpool for Quebec, and there were no survivors.

Outward-bound vessels frequently negotiated the treacherous channels of the Hoyle only to be driven back and destroyed a day or two later, as in the hurricane which began at about midnight on 6 January 1839. The New York packet ship *Pennsylvania* had been anchored off Hoylake since Christmas Day, waiting for a favourable wind, and weighed anchor at 10.30 am on Sunday 6 January. The Liverpool-owned *Lockwoods,* also bound for New York with eighty-five emigrants on board, left at noon, followed two hours later by the American-owned *St Andrew,* a ship of some notoriety among the cotton merchants of New Orleans. By midnight the *Pennsylvania* had passed Point Lynas, the *Lockwoods* was off the Great Orme and the *St Andrew* was beating somewhere off Rhyl when the wind suddenly changed, building up to a south-westerly hurricane by 2.00 am on Monday. It was then that the North West lightship *Planet* (authorised under an Act of 1813), was driven from her moorings and two inward-bound vessels, the *Brighton* and the New York packet *Oxford,* ran aground. The fourteen-

(above) Outward bound from Liverpool in 1898, the SS **Dahomey** encountered thick fog off Holyhead and ran aground at Porth Namarch; (below) after a collision in the Irish Sea in 1910 the SS Star of New Zealand *arrived at Holyhead down by the head and in a sinking condition.*

The ill-fated Rhoscolyn lifeboat Ramon Cabrera *on her final service to the Glasgow steamer* Kirkwynd *which was later refloated.*

Seen unloading cargo close by Bangor Pier is the Christina *which spent many years tramping between Liverpool and Caernarfon. She carried most of the material for the pier's construction in 1896 and collided with it five years later after damaging her propeller near Menai Bridge.*

The PS Rhos Neigr, *down by the bows as she began to sink off Rhos-on-Sea in 1908. Her paddle wheels could still be seen at low tide until the mid-1990s, when they were removed by Trinity House, together with the long-familiar wreck buoy.*

The barnacle- encrusted paddles of the Rhos Neigr were still visible at low tide until the mid 1990s.

man crew of the *Brighton,* which was returning from Bombay, took to a raft but all were drowned.

The three outward-bound ships drifted throughout Monday and at dawn on Tuesday the captain of the *Lockwoods* recognised the Cumberland coast. After some skilful tacking he was again off the Great Orme at 10.00am when all three ships came within sight of each other, and all three captains decided to try to return to Liverpool for repairs to their rigging. While looking for the missing lightship, all three ran on to the Hoyle with less than half-a-mile between them. Fifty-two emigrants and one of the crew of the *Lockwoods* were swept away or died in the rigging as the ship broke up opposite Leasowe; fifteen, including the captain died aboard the *Pennsylvania,* which was a total loss; but all were saved from the *St Andrew.* 'The year 1839 has been as disastrous to the New York packet ships as the whole twenty years preceding have been,' said the *New York Gazette & Commercial Advertiser* in their issue of 13 February.

Americans had good reason to be familiar with the name of the *St Andrew,* following a particularly fast crossing in 1834 when she arrived at New York on Christmas Eve with news of a sharp rise in the price of cotton in Lancashire. One of her owners was banker Nathaniel Prime, who soon produced letters of credit for a million dollars which he gave to a special messenger with instructions to buy up all the Southern cotton he could lay his hands on. Blending bribery with prodigious energy, the messenger got to New Orleans in eleven days – two days ahead of the *Great Southern Mail* from New York. Quietly he bought up 50,000 bales which made a profit of $1^1/2$ million dollars when resold at New York for delivery to Liverpool.

One of the worst emigrant ship disasters of the Welsh coast was the burning of the *Ocean Monarch* off Colwyn Bay on 24 August 1848, with the loss of 178 lives. 'We were then about six miles east of the Great Orme,' reported Capt Murdoch when he came ashore.

> The steward of the ship came up and told me that one of the passengers had lit a fire in one of the ventilators in the afterpart of the ship.... I at once went below and discovered smoke proceeding into the main cabin, through one of the after state-rooms. We began without delay to throw water down; but in five minutes afterwards, indeed almost instantly, the after part of the ship burst into flames.

Later, Capt Murdoch denied that this was how the fire had started, adding that he attributed it to pipe smoking among the steerage passengers, of whom there were 322 on board as well as thirty-two first and second-class cabin passengers. Another survivor attributed the fire to the careless use of a candle by one of the crew of forty-two who was seen entering a locked provision store containing spirits and straw. Whatever the cause, the flames were observed not only from various headlands but also from several vessels which went to the assistance of the *Ocean Monarch,* a ship of 1,300 tons, registered at Boston. First to arrive on the scene was the *Queen of the Ocean,* a yacht owned by Mr Thomas Littledale, Commodore of the Royal Mersey Yacht Club. He was on his way home from Beaumaris regatta and picked up thirty-two survivors before being joined by the Brazilian navy steam frigate *Affonso,* which had just been completed at Birkenhead, the paddler *Prince of Wales,* belonging to the City of Dublin Steam Packet Co, and the outward-bound New York packet ship *New World.* The fire-stricken ship lay at anchor heading into the wind, thus keeping some of the heat of the advancing flames away from the bows where the survivors were gathered and from where the *Affonso* took off 156, while the Prince de Joinville, exiled son of the King of France, sketched the scene.

The *Ocean Monarch* blazed for twenty-four hours and the flames were down to water level before the ship sank by the stern, on the afternoon of 25 August. As the wreck broke up on

The Glasgow motor vessel Emerald was blown ashore while making for one of the two quarry piers at Llanddulas, on 25 February 1974.

the seabed her scorched figurehead drifted free to float ashore a few days later at Rhos-on-Sea. It was taken to Mochdre to be used as a wall decoration in the Mountain View Hotel, then under construction, and there it died of old age many decades later. The *Prince of Wales* paddled on to become one of the original fleet of the Liverpool, Llandudno & Welsh Coast Steam Boat Co when they took over the North Wales services of the City of Dublin Steam Packet Co in 1881. She is not to be confused with a steamer of the same name which was involved in two mishaps in Liverpool Bay three days after the burning of the *Ocean Monarch*, first striking and sinking the Liverpool sloop *Jane* off Rhyl and later herself running aground at Point of Ayr with the loss of the mate and two hands.

Such disasters had little effect on emigration via Liverpool. Shipping losses along the coast of Britain during 1852 added up to 1,115, made up of 500 vessels totally wrecked, 33 lost by collision, and the rest seriously damaged. During 1853 a staggering total of 516 emigrant ships left Liverpool with 203,720 passengers for the United States, very many of them from Wales. During the same period 21,067 emigrants left Liverpool for Australia.

Rhyl's first lifeboat was provided by the Shipwrecked Fishermen & Mariners' Society and appears to have been an unsuccessful American entry for the 1851 competition sponsored by the RNLI in an attempt to find the ideal all-purpose boat. Little is known of its history apart from its condemnation in 1852 as being 'quite unsuitable, under her present form, for the general purposes of a lifeboat on any part of the coast of this country'. The Society promptly replaced it with one of James Beeching's unpopular prize-winning design which, in October 1852, rescued the crew of an un-named vessel wrecked in the Towyn area. When this lifeboat capsized, with the loss of six lives, on 23 January 1853, the whole self-righting principle was challenged by two Welshmen, Henry Richardson, of Aber Hirnant, near Bala, Merioneth, and his son Henry Thomas Richardson, of Brynhyfryd, Pwllheli, Caernarvonshire. Both in the 1851 competition and at the Great Exhibition of the same year they had advocated a design which would now be called a catamaran but which they described as a 'tubular lifeboat'. When the RNLI took over the Rhyl station in 1854 they provided the resort with the first of three Richardson-pattern boats which remained a peculiar feature of Rhyl until 1939.

Having tossed her fateful way across the pages of Welsh history, bestowing her notoriety upon the cyclone which sank her, the *Royal Charter* has almost erased the memory of her launching fiasco at the Sandycroft ironworks, four miles down river from Chester. Huge crowds gathered on the banks of the Dee to witness the intended sideways launch in 1855 but at the appointed hour the 336ft long steam clipper refused to move. After several weeks of costly excavation the *Royal Charter* was floated off her stocks on 31 August – and when six miles down river she struck a sandbank opposite Flint. She had a badly bent keel by the time she was refloated and had to be towed to Liverpool for extensive repairs.

Lifeboat disasters are particularly tragic. Eleven of the crew of the Liverpool Steam-tug Co's lifeboat were drowned while trying to go to the aid of the ship *Cherokee* wrecked on the West Hoyle on 18 February 1854. All thirteen members of the crew were drowned when Point of Air lifeboat capsized off Rhyl on 4 January 1857. Seven of the crew of *Liverpool No 1* lifeboat were lost when the cutter-rigged paddle steamer *Lelia*, 1,100 tons, sank in the same area on 14 January 1865. Nominally commanded by a British master, Capt Skinner, the *Lelia* was actually under instructions from one of her passengers, Capt Arthur Sinclair, of the Confederate States Navy. Her declared cargo was 700 tons of coal for Bermuda, where she was intended to take on a more valuable consignment for Wilmington, North Carolina. Meeting rough weather off the Great Orme the master ordered the anchors to be taken inboard. During this operation one of the anchors was caught by a heavy wave, causing a fluke to penetrate the deck and dislodge an iron scuttle-cover which was washed overboard. Seemingly no one appreciated the seriousness of the damage until the ship failed to answer her helm because of the enormous weight of water in her forepart. Shipping water the whole time, she began to drift eastwards until she foundered when about six miles from the North West lightship. Eighteen of her crew, including Capt Skinner, were lost and twenty-two survivors got to the lightship in two of the *Lelia's* boats. Three of the crew of *No 1* lifeboat also swam to the safety of the lightship when their vessel capsized as they were endeavouring to collect the *Lelia's* survivors.

Welsh-owned vessels, familiar though their masters might be with the coastline, were no less susceptible to the hazards of Liverpool Bay. There was the Nefyn sloop *Pheasant,* lost near New Brighton in 1868; the Caernarfon sloop *Jane & Mary,* wrecked on Rhyl Bar in 1869; the Nefyn schooner *Luther,* lost by collision in the Mersey, 1870; the Aberdyfi sloop *Prosperity,* wrecked off Hoylake, 1871; the Nefyn schooner *Alice,* lost north of Prestatyn, 1873; the Porthmadog smack *Caroline,* which vanished after leaving Mostyn in 1874; the Bangor sloop *Thomas & Ann* lost off Leasowe, 1876; the Abergele pleasure boat *Eagle,* wrecked at Llanddulas, 1876; the Pwllheli sloop *Ruby,* lost on Liverpool Bar, 1876; the Bangor smack *Port Penrhyn,* lost off Hoylake, 1877; and the Porthmadog schooner *Marie Kaestner,* lost without trace after leaving Liverpool for her home port in 1878.

Britain's first submarine, the *Resurgam,* still lies in shallow water off Rhyl. This forgotten steam vessel was invented by a Liverpool curate, the Rev George William Garrett, BA, who began experimenting with a scale model in 1878. His final design was for a hull 41ft long, comprising two iron cones at either end of a tubular-shaped iron section with a 6ft 6in internal diameter but encased in wood to give an overall beam of 9ft 6in. The central section was extended upwards with a small superstructure and central conning tower to give a total depth of a little more than 12ft and a displacement of 30-tons. She was built at the Birkenhead yard of J. T. Cochran & Co, who launched her with a crane into what was then the Great Float (now East and West Floats).

After trials enshrouded in secrecy at the Alfred Dock the Admiralty expressed interest in the invention and, in the darkness of Wednesday evening 10 December 1879, the *Resurgam* set out for Portsmouth. Her crew comprised Mr George Price, as engineer down below, Mr Garrett at the helm in the conning tower, and Capt Jackson keeping a lookout on the outside. The full story of the *Resurgam* has never been told but among the papers of Mr J. T. Cochran was found the following description of the maiden voyage by Mr Garrett:

> As soon as we were in the Rock Channel Captain Jackson came inside when we shut ourselves up and fairly started on our way... we moved about, testing various parts of our intenal machinery, till the Friday morning, when the sun rose beautiful and clear.
>
> We had now been at sea about 36 hours, a great part of which time we were under water, and we felt desirous of making some port as sleeping on board was not attended with as much comfort as we wished. At the time we found the North West lightship close at hand, bearing about North, so we determined to put into the river Foryd as there is good anchorage there, and she will dry every tide, which is very convenient, as we are going to make a series of further experiments. The boat answered splendidly in the seaway. The seas pass easily over her and cause hardly any motion, nor do they interfere in any important degree with her way or steering.

Using the Foryd harbour as their base, the three-man crew experimented for several weeks. Satisfied with the *Resurgam's* submersible qualities, Garrett hired a steam yacht to tow her to Portsmouth. They left Rhyl on 24 February 1880, but within hours were being tossed about in a gale, somewhere off the Great Orme. The steamer's engine failed, and Garrett and his companions abandoned the submarine. No one really knows what happened after that. The *Resurgam* began to sink and then the tow broke. The Admiralty lost interest in the project, and the curate went into partnership with the Swedish machine-gun inventor Thorsten

HMS **Thetis** *beached at Traeth Bychan still with 99 bodies on board, after five months on the seabed off Llandudno.*

HMS Thetis *after being raised (above) and beached at Traeth Bychan. Her bows (right) show the torpedo tubes which caused the disaster. An outer door was open when the inner door was opened. The error caused all future submarine tubes to be fitted with what is known as "the Thetis valve."*

The Vigilant *on station by the keel of HMS* Thetis.

Nordenfelt. Garrett had a narrow escape in 1887, when demonstrating a Nordenfelt submarine to the Turkish navy at Constantinople, and little more was heard of him until he died in
New York, in 1902. In recent years the Royal Navy has cooperated in several attempts to
locate the *Resurgam,* in the hope of making her live up to her name, meaning: 'I shall rise'.

Abergele lifeboat station was opened in 1868 but because of difficulty in finding a crew the
boat was stored at the Foryd, Rhyl, from where it was towed to Llanddulas in 1869, when the
Abergele station was closed without having launched a boat. The quarrymen of Llanddulas
had a life-saving tradition from as long ago as December 1845 when a man named Richard
Thomas, of Conwy, earned the praise of the RNLI for saving the crew of a vessel called the
Richard which was driven ashore near the quarry pier. In 1886 the lifeboat coxswain was
awarded the RNLI silver medal for rescuing the crew of a Swedish-built ketch, the *Dido C* of
Runcorn. An echo of the Llandudno lifeboat mutiny of 7 November 1890 was heard at
Llanddulas where three quarrymen and a shopkeeper were awarded RNLI silver medals for
rescuing the crew of the Padstow schooner *Ocean Queen.* Driven across Colwyn Bay with her
topsails torn to ribbons, the schooner struck Penmaenhead and then drifted on, to settle
down about 150 yd offshore of the old quarry. Through the sleet four men were seen to climb
into the rigging but it was impossible to launch the lifeboat. Five times in three hours the

A Sailor tapping signals to the sinking submarine HMS Thetis.

quarrymen waded up to their necks in efforts to launch a small rowing boat, but each time it was hurled ashore. A telegraph message appealing for Llandudno lifeboat brought back the message that she was already on service to the *Planet;* a second appeal produced the reply that the lifeboat was unfit for launching but that a volunteer crew would be sent by train. Meanwhile the rowing boat was launched for a sixth time and succeeded in reaching the schooner.

One of the victims of this storm of 6/7 November 1890 was Capt Sam Lawrence, a prominent missionary of the British & Foreign Sailors' Society. The weather was already deteriorating on the 5th when Capt Lawrence held a prayer meeting on board his schooner *Glynne* at Connahs Quay. To a visiting sailor who spoke of the danger ahead Capt Lawrence replied: 'What is drowning? Only a mouthful of salt water and glory.' Twenty-four hours later the *Glynne* sailed from the Dee and vanished. Capt Lawrence's father, also a sea captain and a member of the Bethel Union of Christian Shipmasters, who worked from Falmouth, was lost in similar circumstances three years later.

Burning of the emigrant ship **Ocean Monarch** *in 1848.*

Rhyl pier was 785yd long when built in 1867. It lost 60yd when the Chester schooner *Lady Stuart* collided with it on 12 December 1883 – two of the crew saving themselves by jumping on to the landward half as their vessel ploughed through the tangle of cast-iron and timber. Another two were saved by lifeboat. Fifty passengers were rescued by lifeboat when the old paddle steamer *Fawn* struck the pier on 31 August 1891, soon after her acquisition by the Rhyl & Vale of Clwyd Steamship Co. Other North Wales pleasure steamers in trouble before the end of the century were the *St Elvies, St Tudno* and *Hercules,* and all on the same day, 19 September 1896. The *St Elvies,* a 566-ton 18-knot paddler which had only been delivered that summer, was leaving the Mersey with 250 passengers when, in clear weather, she sliced through the rival 153-ton *Hercules* anchored near New Brighton. Although built as a tug, the *Hercules* provided a regular excursion service to Llandudno for the Snowdon Passenger Steamship Co. She sank immediately but eight of her crew of nine were rescued by the badly damaged *St Elvies,* which then disembarked her passengers at New Brighton floating pier. The *St Tudno* was at anchor in the Mersey when struck a glancing blow by an inward-bound ship.

In retrospect, one can acknowledge that the North Wales pleasure steamers had a good safety record. After the loss of the *Rothsay Castle* in 1831 their worst accident was the sinking of the *Rhos Neigr* on 20 July 1908. Her skeleton, including the framework of her paddles, could be seen until the mid-1990s at Rhos-on-Sea. She was built as the *Prince Leopold* in 1876, for service between Southampton and the Isle of Wight, but had worked for the Colwyn Bay & Liverpool Steamship Co from 1905 until a month before her final voyage when she was sold to Capt Walter Hawthorn, of Rhyl.

Capable of carrying 436 passengers, the 196-ton *Rhos Neigr* left Llandudno pier with eighty who had paid half-a-crown (12$\frac{1}{2}$p) for a return trip to Blackpool. Another seventy-five eager holidaymakers were waiting to join her at Rhos-on-Sea pier, and for all these, plus a crew of nineteen, there were only two small lifeboats on board. Paddling along a familiar course at ten knots on a calm day the *Rhos Neigr* was midway between Llandudno and Rhos-on-Sea when Capt Smallman heard 'a sudden grinding noise' from somewhere below the waterline. Going below to investigate, he found water pouring into the foreward half. He ordered the sealing of all bulkheads as he headed for Rhos pier but was 350 yd short of his destination when he realised he would never make it. Slowly turning the sluggish paddler to starboard, and sounding a continuous blast of distress on his siren, he ran his ship aground some 200 yd from the beach. The ship's lifeboats were supplemented by two from her sister paddler, the *Rhos Trevor,* which happened to be anchored nearby, and all the passengers were ferried ashore.

Four hours later, at 2.30 pm, the *Rhos Neigr* refloated on the rising tide and swung round a little, but at 3.00 pm she suddenly dropped by the bows and the crew were ordered to abandon ship. Within a minute the stern had sunk to the bottom, sucking down the owner, Capt Hawthorn, who was fortunate enough to be blown to the surface in an air bubble seconds later. Capt Smallman indignantly denied he could have struck a rock off the Little Orme, while Capt Hawthorn was equally adamant that a baulk of timber could not have been driven through the hull by one of the paddles, since both wheels were intact. There the mystery rests as successive generations of holiday-makers added their theories to the debate on the cause of the picturesque wreck visible from the promenade for the next 90 years.

When next a vessel was lost at Rhos-on-Sea, on 27 March 1919, Coxswain John Owen, of Llandudno lifeboat, was awarded the RNLI bronze medal, the citation reading: 'Whilst the lifeboat was on her way to the wreck she was three times buried by the seas, and on one occasion the men were only saved from being washed overboard by clinging to the lifelines.' It was for the rescue of the crew of the *Ada Mary,* which had lost her sails off the Little Orme while on passage from Ireland to Hoylake with a cargo of timber. Unable to return to Llandudno against a north-westerly gale the lifeboat was beached at Colwyn Bay.

Llandudno lifeboat's most harrowing launch was on Friday 2 June 1939 when she took a doctor fourteen miles into Liverpool Bay to the spot where ninety-nine men were slowly dying in the doomed submarine HMS *Thetis.* 'I was summoned to the scene of the disaster after four men had escaped,' said Dr A. Maddock Jones who had answered the Navy's 'SOS' from his surgery on the promenade near the lifeboat slipway. 'It was probably felt that others would come up from the submarine but they did not. I waited throughout the day but unfortunately my services were not needed,' he added. Five days later the lifeboat returned to the scene to cast a wreath upon the waves while a bugler sounded the Last Post from the quarterdeck of HMS *Hebe.*

HMS Thetis, *beached at Traeth Bychan, five months after failing to surface from her first test dive in Liverpool Bay.*

Thetis, the third of the new 'T' class submarines ordered for the Royal Navy in 1936, left the Birkenhead yards of Cammell Laird at 9.40 am on Thursday 1 June. There were 103 mixed naval and civilian personnel, including a Mersey pilot, on board for her first diving test. Her only escort was the 169-ton Liverpool tug *Grebecock*, which was carrying a young naval liaison officer and a telegraphist who, at 4.45 pm sent his first radio message to Submarine Headquarters at Fort Blockhouse, Gosport: 'What was duration of *Thetis* dive?' Although unrecognised as such, this was an early warning from Lt R. E. Coltart that all was not well in Liverpool Bay. He had not been too happy about the way in which *Thetis* had dived, commencing at 2.00 pm and taking fifty-eight minutes to overcome her buoyancy before suddenly plunging beneath the surface. Slowly making its way through civilian channels, the message arrived at Gosport Post Office while the telegram boy was mending a puncture on his bicycle, so that it was 6.15 pm before it got to Fort Blockhouse. It confirmed the apprehension already felt at Submarine HQ from where, at ten-minute intervals, attempts had been made to call up *Thetis* by radio since 4.45 pm. Within seven minutes of Lt Coltart's simple message reaching its destination various units of the Navy were on their way to Liverpool Bay.

Meanwhile frustration and anxiety were mounting on board the *Grebecock*. Attempts to send a more urgent message having failed because of the low power of the radio equipment, Lt Coltart and Mr A. E. Godfrey, the master of the tug, debated whether they should run for Llandudno to summon assistance, or stay where they were both to mark the position and to pick up any men who might escape with Davis apparatus. In fact, by having to rely upon compass, chart and calculations of tidal speed, the *Grebecock* had drifted four miles to the north of the diving position where the *Thetis* was eventually found. By way of added complication, the *Grebecock* had anchored thirteen miles west of where she said she was when contact was made with the approaching rescue fleet. In failing light, an RAF Anson spotted the distress buoy released by the *Thetis* and calculated its position to be about a mile south of where it actually was. Unfortunately the RAF crew decided to recalculate the position and gave a new and seemingly authoritative position which was seven miles south of true.

The *Thetis* was eventually found at 7.54 am on Friday by the destroyer, HMS *Brazen*. Eighteen feet of the submarine's stern was protruding from the sea at an angle of 40° from horizontal and a few minutes later the trapped men heard a series of twelve underwater detonations telling them that help had arrived. It was decided that two men should try to reach the surface via the submarine escape chamber so as to help organise the rescue, and those chosen to go were Capt H.P. K. Oram, a veteran submariner, and Lt Frederick Woods, the torpedo officer, who would be able to explain how the *Thetis* had flooded for'ard through faulty drill in the use of a torpedo tube. Both officers were picked up by the *Brazen* which, by this time, had been joined by the Mersey Docks & Harbour Board salvage ship *Vigilant*. While a wire rope was being passed under the stem of the *Thetis* one man scrambled on to her with a hammer to tap out the Morse message: 'Come out'. Alas, the men below, weakened by carbon dioxide poisoning, were having difficulty with the escape equipment and only two more got away.

Captain Andrew Flint, master of the Bobara, *comes ashore near Holyhead by breeches buoy, a feature of North Wales coast rescue equipment since 1815.*

The coaster Red Hand which capsized and sank at the mouth of the Dee estuary when her cargo of iron ore shifted in 1927.

A seven-horse team was used to launch the Llanddulas lifeboat, here seen with her crew and helpers about 1909.

With the rising tide the wire rope connecting the *Vigilant* and the *Thetis* snapped and the submarine was not seen again until beached at Traeth Bychan, near Moelfre, five months later. Her dead were taken to Holyhead for burial and the submarine was returned to Cammell Laird from whose yard she re-emerged in November 1940 as HMS *Thunderbolt*. She sank two German submarines and five supply ships before herself being destroyed by depth charges from the Italian corvette *Cicogna*, north of Sicily, on 13 March 1943.

North Wales was the scene of the world's first hovercraft wreck. It happened at Rhyl where a Vickers Armstrong VA-3 had been moored to await a tug after a successful experimental season pioneering a regular 60-knot passenger service between Hoylake and Rhyl. During a storm soon after midnight on 17 September 1962 the crew found that their lightweight mooring points were being torn away and they put to sea in an attempt to prevent the hovercraft being driven ashore. On learning there were three men aboard the VA-3, Mr Harold Campini, coxswain of Rhyl lifeboat, decided to launch.

A spring tide driven before a west-north-westerly gale had flooded the promenade lifeboat house to a depth of 4ft, something never known before or since. 'It was an incredible sight. We manoeuvred the carriage only a few yards and launched straight off the promenade,' recalled local lifeboat secretary Mr John Owen – a veteran of the salvage of the *Lucellum* twenty-one years earlier. 'As she came clear of the carriage the boat rose almost vertically and then dropped sideways with a huge crash into a trough. Fortunately the boat had enough way on to bring her head round and make for the hovercraft,' he added. The amphibian was found drifting and swirling in the dark towards the promenade wall to the east of the boathouse. Coxswain Campini managed to get alongside long enough for the crew to jump to safety and seven minutes later the 25-ton hovercraft, carrying 250 gallons of aviation fuel, was wrecked. Mr Campini received the RNLI silver medal for this historic rescue.

The RNLI medal for gallantry at sea.

INTO THE
21ST CENTURY

THE 21st century will hopefully see Britain's first powered submarine, the *Resurgam,* living up to her name, which translates as "I shall rise." She sank in 1880, off the Great Orme while in tow from Rhyl for Naval testing at Portsmouth. For more than a century she evaded countless attempts to locate her, including several expeditions by the Royal Navy, on behalf of their Submarine Museum, at Gosport.

The submarine inventor's American great grandson, Bill Garrett, turned up at Rhyl in June 1989, to finance and supervise a week-long search. "There have been searches for the past eight years by people hired by the Royal Navy Submarine Museum – all of them in the wrong place," said Bill Scanlon Murphy, the historical advisor for the search. "We, on the other hand, have simply gone back to the original documents and seen where the crew said she was when she sank. We have a precise location and are confident of finding the *Resurgam,*" he added. Alas, this expedition was no more successful than all the others. The tidal pattern of this coast had gradually bounced the *Resurgam* back to within eight miles of Rhyl.

In October 1995 Rhyl trawler skipper Dennis Hunt snagged and lost his net while fishing in Liverpool Bay, where the murky shallow sea bed is littered with the debris of Victorian mishaps. The same sort of thing had happened many times before, and next day Mr Hunt asked 41-years-old amateur diver Keith Hurley to help him recover the net, as he had done in the past.

"I wasn't expecting to see anything apart from rubbish on the sea bed, but then I saw a shoal of fish, suggesting there was a wreck, and like a flash of a camera there it was *Resurgam,*" said Mr Hurley. "She was still in one piece, from one pointed end to the other, apart from a massive gash in her hull. There, too, was the rudimentary conning tower gaping upwards like the mouth of some monstrous sea creature," he said. The vessel was simply sitting on the sea bed, in shallow water, covered in barnacles and sea growth but instantly recognisable.

Back on the surface Mr Hurley found the world reluctant to believe he had found the elusive *Resurgam* but he telephoned Mr Garrett, in New Jersey, who flew to Britain. Mr Hurley sought to keep the location secret to protect the wreck from souvenir hunters, and so Mr Garrett commissioned a survey vessel which relocated the *Resurgam,* and confirmed she was in reasonably good condition. It is thought the presence of this vessel alerted the amateur diving fraternity. The Royal Navy initiated an Historic Wreck Site Order, which outlaws unauthorised interference with the vessel, and CADW, the State body responsible for Welsh historic monuments, granted an excavation licence to the Resurgam Trust, but such measures do not inhibit diving adventurers. In September 2000 Martin Dean, of the Archaeological Diving Unit at St. Andrews' University, reported the wreck of the *Resurgam* had been lifted and dropped some 30ft from her 1995 location, and turned through 90 degrees, something that might have been done with air bags. She appeared to have been damaged in the process. Meanwhile the world argues about the future fate of the *Resurgam* – the Resurgam Trust is hoping the Heritage Lottery Fund will finance her resurfacing, but others say that is too slow a process to save her from maritime vandals.

In recognition of her inventor's Welsh link Bill Garrett ordered a tombstone of Welsh slate to be shipped to America at the end of 2000, bearing the inscription:

Resurgam, 1879, sacred to the memory of Rev. George
William Garrett, born London 1852. died NYC 1902.
Father of the Submarine.

Another lost submarine which has been attracting interest among maritime historians is the Royal Navy's *H5*, rammed in Caernarfon Bay on 2 March 1918. She was patrolling the area at night when spotted on the surface by the SS *Rutherglen*. Unable to identify the submarine, and unwilling to risk the consequences of challenging a German U-boat, the officers of the *Rutherglen* exercised their discretion, allowing them to ram any vessel they did not recognise. The Canadian-built submarine was lost with all 27 of her crew and the Admiralty rewarded the *Rutherglen's* crew with the customary bounty for sinking an enemy U-boat — deliberately choosing not to tell them they had sunk a Royal Navy vessel. One of the *H5's* crew was Earl Childs, the first American submariner to be killed in action, and who was posthumously honoured by having a US Navy destroyer named after him. That destroyer earned a battle star when seeking to defend the fleet attacked by the Japanese at Pearl Harbour in 1941.

The Ellerman Line's SS *Castilian*, sunk in 1943, began causing problems in 1987, when amateur divers were found to be stealing her cargo of anti-aircraft shells, in order to salvage the brass shell cases, worth about £30 each in the scrap metal trade. The ship had been found, upside down, in about 120ft of water, half-a-mile off the Skerries lighthouse. Police called in explosives experts when they found that thieves had been bringing complete shell assemblies ashore, where the shell and cordite propellant were extracted and dumped, on one of Anglesey's most popular beaches, in an area designated as being of outstanding natural beauty.

"We have not yet made a complete survey of the wreck but we believe there are thousands of tons of explosives down there, as well as a few Jeeps and some rolling stock," said Lieutenant-Commander Stuart Harper, who brought a team of naval divers to begin removing the cargo for controlled destruction.

"Diving conditions are not at their best in the area because there is a mass of water moving at up to eight or nine miles an hour, and we are able to work only when the weather is good. It will be a long job," said Lt-Cdr Harper. It was decided not to blow up the entire ship (which had broken into three parts) because of its proximity to the lighthouse, and the Navy was still removing explosive in 1996, when Parliament was told the operation would be completed by the end of the year.

A more benign diving discovery in 1979 was the *Ocean Monarch*, off Colwyn Bay. The 1,300-ton ship had safely rounded Anglesey and the Great Orme for the last stretch of her voyage from Boston to Liverpool when she caught fire in August 1848. She burnt for 15 hours before sinking. There were 352 passengers and a crew of 42 on board, and 178 lost their lives.

The wreck was found 131 years later by Rhyl fisherman John Povah, who accidentally salvaged some of her scattered inscribed crockery in his fishing net. He subsequently dived on the wreck with friends, who spoke of a giant lobster, weighing an estimated 16lbs, which lived in the hull, and which they named Eric.

There was a flurry of diving activity off the *Ocean Monarch* in 1987 — bringing about the wrecking of the *Grampian Castle*. The divers were looking for her 420 cases of crockery, despite Mr Povah's belief that most of it would have been destroyed by fire or subsequent problems. The divers' first salvage vessel, the *Grampian Castle*, was seeking shelter in the

Rhos-on-Sea acquired an unexpected tourist attraction on 28 September 1991, when the 500-ton Marga, of Cortes, Honduras, was blown ashore after dragging her anchors while waiting for fair weather off Llanddulas. She was later hauled back to sea.

Wr. 42.

ISSUED BY THE
BOARD OF TRADE.

NOTICE.

WRECKED PROPERTY.

To Fishermen, Boatmen, and other Persons who may find Wrecked Property.

The Merchant Shipping Acts, 1894 and 1906, provide that if any person, not being the owner, finds or takes possession of wreck he shall, as soon as possible, deliver it to the Receiver of Wreck or the nearest Customs and Excise or Coast Guard Officer and that if he omits to do so he shall be liable to the following penalties:—

A fine not exceeding £100.
Forfeiture of all claims to salvage and
Payment to the owner of the wreck of double its value.

NOTE.—Wreck includes all cargo and other articles belonging to any vessel stranded or in distress on the shore or in any tidal waters of the United Kingdom, or picked up at sea and brought within the United Kingdom.

BOARD OF TRADE,
October 1915.

RHYBUDD.

EIDDO LLONGDDRYLLIAD.

AT BYSGOTWYR, BADWYR, A PHERSONAU ERAILL A DDICHON GAEL EIDDO LLONGDDRYLLIAD.

Deddfau Masnach Morawl, 1894 a 1906, a ddywed--Unrhyw berson heb fod y perchennog a gaiff neu a gymer i'w feddiant eiddo Llongddrylliad y rhaid iddo, cynted a bo modd, roddi'r cyfryw i fyny i Dderbynydd Eiddo Llongddrylliad, neu i'r Swyddog agosaf o'r Dollfa a'r Cyllid neu i Swyddog y Glannau, ac os esgeulusa wneuthur hyny bydd yn agored i'r dirwyon canlynol:—

Dirwy heb fod dros £100.
Colli pob hawl o wobr am achub a.
Thâl i berchen y gweddillion o'i werth yn ddau cymaint.

SYLW.—Cynhwysa Llongddrylliad bob eiddo a berthyn i unrhyw long yrrwyd ar y traeth, neu sydd mewn cyfyngder ar y glanau neu o fewn unrhyw dufr llanw o'r Deyrnas Gyfunol, neu a godwyd i fyny o'r mor ac a ddygwyd i'r Deyrnas Gyfunol.

BWRDD MASNACH,
Hydref, 1915.

Printed for H.M. Stationery Office by Wyman's London Printing Co., Ltd., Elm Street, W.C.1   2652. Wt. 21526/8197. 250. 11/33. **(613)**.

Menai Strait when on its way to Colwyn Bay in March 1987, but ran aground on Caernarfon Bar. She was replaced by the *Bntish Enterprise V* which spent ten days over the wreck in May.

"Eric the lobster no longer lives there," said Mr Povah after the visiting divers left. "Local people who dived on the wreck had all said we would never touch the lobster, but he hasn't been seen since they first started diving there. I am told a lobster of that size might have been living in the wreck for a hundred years," he added.

Four years later Caernarvon Harbourmaster Captain Emlyn Jones said he was investigating complaints about the abandoned wreck of the *Grampian Castle,* which several small boats reported having hit. He said its mast was visible above high water level and the whole hull was visible at low tide, so there was no reason for running into it with modern craft.

The lure of gold sovereigns continues to attract fortune hunters to the wreck of the *Royal Charter,* near Moelfre. There was a major expedition in 1985 but in October 1987 the venture ended up in the courts, the partners went their separate ways, and Anglesey people were still seeking payment for 1985 bills.

One of the most interesting wreck discoveries off the North Wales coast began with the 1978 sighting of two large cannon off Talybont, in Cardigan Bay, by members of Glaslyn Sub-Aqua Club. It took a long time to find the site a second time, aided by Harlow branch of BSAC, one of whom later reported: "The seabed is littered with cannon of various sizes, some as large as nine feet long, but generally of two sizes, indicating a double-decked ship. A very interesting bronze bell in superb condition was found, and brought to the surface. This bears the date 1677, a Latin religious inscription, and several engraved heads.

"In the centre of the wreck area is a large pile of blocks which, after investigation, turned out to be high grade carrera marble. There would appear to be several hundred tons of it. At the bow end of the wreck lie two huge anchors, one with a shaft of about 12ft, and at the stern end lies another large anchor.

"The discovery of some small cannon created great interest and one of these was lifted for identification. It turned out to be a very rare swivel gun of the early 16th century, known as a Verso. When removed from its concretion it was found to be in amazingly good condition. It was loaded and charged, and had the muzzle bung in place."

Subsequently known as the Cae Nest Project, this wreck was made the subject of one of the first Orders under the Protection of Shipwrecks Act 1973, prohibiting unauthorised diving within 150 metres.

A Maltese-registered tanker, the 1,675-ton MV *Kimya,* capsized off Holyhead on 6 January 1991, while on passage from St.Nazaire to Birkenhead with a cargo of sunflower oil. Ten of her crew were lost and two were rescued by RAF helicopter. She remained afloat, upside down, with her superstructure dragging the bottom, and was towed to a sheltered area near Llanddwyn Island. Trinity House made first use of their air portable wreck buoy, which was taken by road from Harwich to RAF Valley, from where a helicopter dropped it into position five days later. At the end of 1992 it was decided to mark the wreck with a permanent buoy, after her flagged owners had gone out of business and their insurers had abandoned it. Trinity House reported in September 1992 that the *Kimya's* cargo tanks were open to the sea and the bunker fuelling points and vent pipes had disappeared. No coastal pollution had occurred and Trinity House were of the view that any remaining oil in the wreck did not pose a threat to the environment.

On 28 September 1991 three ships were anchored off Llanddulas, waiting for storm winds to abate, to enable them to move up to the quarry jetties to take on cargoes of stone. In the dark, one ship, the 500-ton *Marga,* dragged her anchor and was blown ashore at Rhos-on-Sea, causing damage to a wooden jetty and a rock groyne. She was registered at Cortes, in Honduras, and had a crew of only five, none of whom was injured. The *Marga* was high and dry at low tide, providing an unexpected tourist attraction. Salvage tugs were later able to haul her back to sea.

There was similar tourist excitement on Llandudno's West Shore, in October 1987, when a drilling barge was swept ashore. She had been moored in Conwy Harbour during the construction of Britain's first immersed-tube tunnel which now carries the A55/E22 road beneath the estuary. When the storm abated cranes removed some of the barge's equipment, enabling her to be hauled back to sea on a high tide.

A short-lived hovercraft pleasure cruise operation out of Llandudno ended abruptly on 6 August 1990 when the 16-seater craft was swept from her mooring, onto the North Shore. Alerted by a local hotelier, the four owners dashed into the sea to try to save the vessel but one was seriously injured. By the time she came ashore the vessel's wooden propeller had been shredded, the steering system had been smashed, and the superstructure had been ripped open. The wreck was lifted on to a low-loader transporter and taken away. This was the second hovercraft to come to grief on the North Wales coast.

Thirteen people were rescued when the Rhyl fishing boat *June Starfish* began taking in water very quickly in June 1994. The skipper's *M'aidez* (Mayday) radio message to Holyhead Coastguard station was heard by two other fishing boats, the *Golden Dawn* and *Guide Me*, which happened to be in the area, some two miles off shore. "It was sheer good luck that we steered in the right direction," said Ian Parry, owner of the *Golden Dawn*. "Very little of the *June Starfish* was sticking out of the water and when we got there we found scattered people, including four children, clinging to lifebelts and debris. They were cold and weak. One was a very heavy non-swimmer, and it took us 20 minutes to haul him out of the sea," he added.

Two fishermen, Andy Wragg and Steve Dop, spent three hours clinging to a life raft on a bitterly cold night in November 1996, when Mr Wragg's 30ft trawler *Horizon* took in water and sank. She had left Rhos-on-Sea harbour in good weather, and they were some 10 miles off the Great Orme when their radar died. Then the radio began to crackle and finally the engine stopped. The men found water waist deep in the engine room, and the stern began to sink. They took to their life raft and three or four minutes later the *Horizon* sank. Their tenth distress flare was spotted by the captain of the 58,000 ton *Atlantic Conveyor*, as the ship headed for Liverpool. He signalled a response and informed Holyhead Coastguards. The men were found by a RAF helicopter from Valley, which guided Llandudno lifeboat to them. Next day Mr Dop found the overnight storm had also wrecked his own 26ft fishing boat *Blue Tara*, which had dragged from her moorings at Rhos-on-Sea, damaging her hull and rudder before sinking.

There was a strange expedition on Llandudno's West Shore in 1985 when Bob Renphrey took a hack-saw out to the remains of the *Flying Foam* to salvage a piece for his daughter Stella, a granddaughter of the schooner's last owner, Captain Roystone Jackson. "Those who play in what little is left of the *Flying Foam* might like to know something about the colourful Capt. Jackson," said Mr. Renphrey. "He alternated careers on the stage and at sea. He was described as an actor on his marriage certificate in 1918, but had been torpedoed by a U-boat in 1917. He was sentenced to two months imprisonment in November 1918 after being arrested on the stage of the London Palladium for wearing the VC. He was gaoled for bigamy in 1919 and again in 1926. American Prohibition attracted him back to sea as a liquor smuggler, until the US Coastguard sank his ship in 1929. He wrecked a ketch in 1931 and used the insurance money to produce a stage show. He was back at sea in 1933, having to be rescued three times within the year. After a period as a London busker he produced a travelling concert party in 1935. The Spanish Civil War took him back to sea as a blockade runner, in and out of Bilbao with a 240-ton ketch. He also tried his hand as a lion tamer, a preacher and a medium. He died a pauper in 1951 and the wreck of the *Flying Foam* is the only maritime relic we have of him."

BIBLIOGRAPHY

CHAPTER ONE THE AMERICAN GATEWAY

Allen, Thomas	*Lancashire Illustrated,* (1832)
Allison, J. E.	*The Mersey Estuary,* Liverpool, (1949)
Central Office of Information	*The Battle of the Atlantic,* (1946)
Chander, George	*Liverpool Shipping,* (1960)
Hughes, John Morris	*Hanes Methodistiaeth Liverpool, Cyf 1,* Liverpool, (1929)
Lloyd, Christopher	*The British Seaman 1200-1860,* (1970)
MacInnes, C. M.	*Bristol & the slave trade,* Bristol, (1968)
Macintyre, Donald	*The Battle of the Atlantic,* (1961)
Maginnis, A. J.	*The Atlantic Ferry,* (1892)
Marshall, Peter	*The Anti-Slave Trade Movement in Bristol,* Bristol, (1968)
McKay, Richard C.	*Some famous sailing ships, and their builder Donald McKay,* Riverside, Connecticut, (1969)
Mersey Docks & Harbour Board	*Business in Great Waters,* Liverpool, (1958)
Mountfield, Stuart	*Western Gateway,* Liverpool, (1965)
Robertson, Terence	*Walker, R.N.,* (1966)
Thomas, David	*Hen longau a llongwyr Cymru,* Cardiff, (1949)
	Anglesey Marine Terminal Bill, (29 April 1971)
	Mersey Docks & Harbour Board (Anglesey Terminal) Bill, (4 December 1970)
	Shipwrecks & Disasters at Sea, Halifax, (1863)
	Thames & Mersey Marine Insurance Co Ltd, 1860-1960, Liverpool, (1960)

CHAPTER TWO CARDIGAN BAY

Davies, J. Glyn	*Cerddi Huw Puw,* Liverpool, (1923)
Dawson, A. J.	*Britain's Lifeboats,* (1923)
Ellis, W. J.	'The church of St Hywyn, Aberdaron,' *Transactions of Caernarvonshire Historical Society,* (1950)
Evans, Ioan Mai	*Gwlad Llyn,* Llandybie, (1968)
Hughes, Henry	*Immortal Sails,* Prescot, (1969)
Jones, Jennie	*Tomos o Enlli,* Llandybie, (1964)

Lewis, L. Haydn   *Penodau yn hanes Aberaeron a'r cylch*, Llandysul, (1970)
Morgan, D. W.   *Brief Glory*, Liverpool, (1948)
Morris, William   *Plans of harbours, bays & roads in St George's & Bristol
                          Channels*, Shrewsbury, (1801)
Owen, H. J.   *Treasures of the Mawddach*, Dolgellau, (1950)
Parry, Bryn R.   *Caernarvonshire Records*, Caernarfon, (1968)
Thomas, David   *Hen longau Sir Gaernarfon*, Caernarfon, (1952)
Williams, Christopher,   'The Llandudno copper mines,' *Transactions of
                          Caernarvonshire Historical Society*, (1972)
Williams, Peter L.   *History of the Criccieth Lifeboat Station*, Criccieth, (1968)

CHAPTER THREE CAERNARFON BAY: SOUTH

Dodd, O. A.   'Captain and the stowaway,' *Country Quest*, (May 1969)
Hall, Edmund Hyde   *A Description of Caernarvonshire 1809-1811*,
                            Caernarfon, (1952)
Jones, Ivor Wynne   'Attack from the West,' *Liverpool Daily Post*,
                            (14-17 November 1966)
National Maritime Museum   *For Those in Peril*, (1963)
Parry, Henry   *The Lifeboats of Cardigan Bay & Anglesey*, Truro, (1969)
Stubbs, J. M.   'Marine Archaeology,' *Caernarvonshire Record Office
                            Bulletin No 3*, (1970)
Thomas, David   *Hen longau Sir Gaernarfon*, Caernarfon, (1952)
                           Dangers of the Deep, (1848)
                           North Wales Chronicle, (22 April 1830, 29 April 1830,
                            13 May 1830)

CHAPTER FOUR CAERNARFON BAY: NORTH

Bowen, Frank C.   *Sailing Ships of the London River*, nd
Bulkeley, William   *MS diary*, University College of North Wales, Bangor
Farr, Grahame   *The Steamship Great Britain*, Bristol, (1970)
Glazebrook, Henry   *Anglesey & North Wales Coast Book*, Bangor, (1962)
Owen, Hugh   *Hanes Plwyf Niwbwrch ym Môn*, Caernarfon, (1952)
Patterson, J. E.   *A Hero of the Sea*, (1910)
Rowland, K. T.   *The Great Britain*, Newton Abbot, (1971)
Salmon, P. J.   'Saga of the Norman Court,' *Sea Breezes*, (May 1969)
Vincent, J. E. (ed)   *The Memories of Sir Llewelyn Turner*, (1903)
William, Dafydd Wyn   'Lladron Crigyll,' *Môn*, (Gaeaf 1968-9)
                        Caernarvon & Denbigh Herald, (13 March 1870,
                         20 March 1870)
                        Illustrated London News, (2 September 1848, 6 May 1854)

CHAPTER FIVE HOLYHEAD

Anderson, A. O.	letter in *Sea Breezes,* (December 1968)
Archer, Michael Scott	*The Welsh Post Towns before 1840*, Chichester, (1970)
Barnes, F.	*Barrow & district: an illustrated history*, Barrow,(1951)
Bulloch, James D.	*The Secret Service of the Confederate States in Europe*, (1883)
Butterworth, Geoffrey	'The story of Penrhos,' *Môn*, (Winter 1968-9)
Chatterton, E. Keble	*The Epic of Dunkirk*, (1940)
Duckworth, C.L.D. & Langmuir G.E.	*Railway & Other Steamers*, Prescot, (1968)
Dugan, James	*The Great Iron Ship*, (1953)
Goodhart, Philip	*Fifty ships that saved the world*, (1965)
Hughes, D. Lloyd, & Williams, Dorothy M.	*Holyhead The Story of a port*, Holyhead, (1967)
Lenton, H. T. & Colledge, J. J.	*Warships of World War II*, (1970)
McNeill, D. B.	*Irish passenger steamship services, Vol 2*, Newton Abbot, (1971)
Sanderson, Peter E.	'The importance of external factors in the development of the Port of Holyhead *Transactions of Anglesey Antiquarian Society*, (1963)
Smith-Hughes, Jack,	'W. S. Miller & Co of Glasgow,' *Sea Breezes,* (September 1968)
Williams, Huw Llewelyn	*Wrth Angor yn Nulyn*, Caernarfon, (1968)
Williams, Lucy,	'Sea raiders in the waters between Anglesey and Ireland during the 17th and 18th centuries,' *Transactions of the Honourable Society of Cymmrodorion*, (1946)
Yeates, A. Cyril,	'The Holyhead route to Ireland,' *Sea Breezes,* (January 1967)
	'Railway cargo ships of Holyhead,' *Sea Breezes,* (December 1970)
	Archaeologia Cambrensis, (1851)
	Holyhead & Anglesey Mail, (9 Feb 1884, 3 May 1884, 2 Feb 1968)
	Port of Liverpool News, (June 1971)
	Sea Breezes, (March 1971)

CHAPTER SIX NORTHERN ANGLESEY

Aspden, Fred	'The lights that never fail,' *Port of Liverpool News*, (October 1970)
Bishop, Eleanor	'Mr Bulkeley had a pirate in the parlour,' *Country Quest*, (Winter 1963)
Callender, Geoffrey	'The earliest English yachts,' *Illustrated London News*, (3 April 1929)
Challinor, P. J.	*The heritage of Oswestry*, Oswestry, (1962)
Davies, Ivor E.	'Conway's busy waterfront,' *Liverpool Daily Post*, (24 November 1964)

Dickens, Charles	*Uncommercial Traveller,* (1860)
Eames, Aled	'Frances Williams and the Anglesey Association for the Preservation of Life from Shipwreck, 1827-1857,' *Transactions of Anglesey Antiquarian Society,* (1957)
Farr, Grahame	letter in *Sea Breezes,* (February 1970)
Greenhill, Basil	*The Merchant Schooners,* Two vols, Newton Abbot, (1968)
Heaton, Peter	*Yachting, a history,* (1955)
Hughes, T. E.	'Dominion Line's chequered history,' *Sea Breezes,* (April 1971)
Jones, Bedwyr Lewis	'Llongdrylliad y Marchioness of Anglesey,' *Transactions of Anglesey Antiquarian Society,* (1965)
Jones, D. F. V.	'The Amlwch riots of 1817,' *Transactions of Anglesey Antiquarian Society,* (1966)
Lenton, H. T.	*German submarines, Vol 1,* (1965)
Lewis, Keith P.	letter in *Sea Breezes,* (May 1971)
McKay, Richard C.	*South Street: A maritime history of New York,* Riverside, Connecticut, (1969)
McKee, Alexander	*The Golden Wreck,* (1961)
Mead, Hilary P.	*Trinity House,* nd, (c1947)
Powell, Roger	'The port between two rocks,' *Rhwng môr a mynydd,* Llangefni, nd, (c1965)
Roskill, Capt S. W.	*The War at Sea, Vol 3, Part 2,* (1961)
Seely, Major General	*Launch,* (1932)
Ware, Jean	'The Enchanted Isle,' *Country Quest,* (Summer 1962)
	Illustrated London News, (24 August 1850, 4 February 1854)
	Liverpool Daily Post, (17 April 1916, 14 August 1962)
	North Wales Chronicle, (9 December 1830)

CHAPTER SEVEN MENAI STRAIT

Bingley, William	*North Wales,* (1804)
Davies, H. R.	*The Conway & Menai Ferries,* Cardiff, (1942)
Davies, R. W.	*Llythyrau hen forwr,* Liverpool, (1933)
Henry, Fred	*Ships of the Isle of Man Steam Packet Co,* Glasgow, (1967)
Jones, W. H	*Old Karnarvon,* Caernarfon, nd, (c1882)
Masefield, John	*The Conway,* (1953)
Owen, Bob	'Y barque Hindoo.' *Transactions of Caernarvonshire Historical Society,* (1944)
Senogles, David	*The Story of Ynys Gorad Goch,* Menai Bridge, (1969)
Thomas, T. Rees & Jones, J. Pritchard	*Summary of the Statutes & Orders which govern the Caernarvon Harbour Trust,* nd

Thornley, F. C.   *Steamers of North Wales,* Prescot, (1962)
Vincent, J. E. (ed)   *The Memories of Sir Llewelyn Turner,* (1903)
                           Archaeologia Cambrensis, (1851)
                           Centenary of the Indefatigable, Liverpool, (1964);
                           Holyhead & Anglesey Mail, (13 September 1884)

CHAPTER EIGHT CONWY BAY

Hadley, Alice   *Conway Parish Registers,* (1900)
Jones, W.   *The Gwyneddion for 1832,* (1839)
Lewis, E. A.   *The Welsh Port Books 1550-1603,* (1927)
Lockhart, J. G.   *Peril of the Sea,* (1924)
Lowe, W. Bezant,   *The Heart of Northern Wales, Vol 1,* Llanfairfechan, (1912)
Owen, Bob   'Yr ymfudo o Sir Gaernarfon i'r Unol Daleithiau,'
                           Transactions of Caernarvonshire Historical Society, (1952)
Thomas, David   *Hen longau Sir Gaernarfon,* Caernarfon, (1952)
Zanelli, Leo   *Shipwrecks around Britain,* (1970)
                           Llandudno Advertiser, (25 November 1893, 8 October 1896)
                           North Wales Chronicle, (19 December 1968)

CHAPTER NINE GREAT ORME

Eames, Aled   'Sea power and Caernarvonshire, 1642-1660,'
                           Transactions of Caernarvonshire Historical Society, (1955)
Hicklin, John   *Llandudno and its vicinity,* (1856)
James, Rev. J. Spinther   MS history of Llandudno, whereabouts now unknown
Roberts, John, Hanes   *Bedyddwyr cylch Llandudno,* Llandudno (1926)
Rowlands, Thomas   *Adgofion am Llandudno,* Llandudno, (1892)
                           Llandudno Advertiser, (November 1919) (lifeboat history)
                           Memorial of the Provisional Committee of the North
                           Wales & Dublin Railway Co, (1844)
                           North Wales Weekly News, (9 April 1970)

CHAPTER TEN LIVERPOOL BAY

Aspinall, Henry K.   *Birkenhead & its surroundings,* Liverpool, (1903)
Ballantyne, R. M.   *Battles with the sea,* (1883)
Caton, Alice G.   *Romance of Wirral,* Liverpool, (1949)
Dawson, A. J.   *Britain's Lifeboats,* (1923)
Duckworth, C. L. D. &
  Langmuir, G. E.   *West Coast Steamers,* Prescot, (1966)
Eames, Aled   *Llandudno Lifeboat 1861-1961,* Llandudno, (1961)

Evans, Olwen Caradoc	*Marine Plans & Charts of Wales,* (1969)
Fyfe, Herbert C.	*Submarine Warfare,* (1907)
Gamlin, Hilda	*Twixt Mersey & Dee,* Liverpool, (1897)
James, J. W.	*Rhuddlan & its church,* Rhuddlan, (1969)
Jones, Ivor Wynne	'Mystery of the *Rhos Neigr* wreck,' *Liverpool Daily Post,* (15 September 1964)
Jones, Ivor Wynne	'The world's first hovercraft rescue,' *Liverpool Daily Post,* (25 February 1970)
McIntyre, W. R. S.	*Birkenhead yesterday and today,* Liverpool, (1948)
Methley, Noel T.	*The lifeboat and its story,* (1912)
Paget-Tomlinson, E. W.	*The History of the Bibby Line,* Liverpool, (1970)
Parry, Edward	*Railway Companion from Chester to Holyhead,* Chester, (1849, reprinted 1970)
Robinson, H.	*Cheshire river navigations with special reference to the River Dee,* Altrincham, (1967)
Taylor, A. J.	*Rhuddlan Castle,* (1955)
Tucker, Norman	*Colwyn Bay, its origin & growth,* Colwyn Bay, (1953)
Venables-Williams, W.	*An archaeological history of Llandrillo-yn-Rhos,* Colwyn Bay, (1898)
Warren, C. E. T. & Benson, James	*The Admiralty Regrets, (1958)*
Williams, A. H.	*Welsh Wesleyan Methodism 1800-1858,* Bangor, (1935)
Wilson, William	*A century of local government in Wallasey,* Wallasey, (1935)
	'Britain's first submarine,'*Sea Breezes,* (January 1961)
	The Story of Rhyl's lifeboats, Rhyl, (1952)
	Chart & Compass, (March 1892, February 1894)
	Gore's Directory, 1895, reprinted 1971 as 'An everyday history of Liverpool.'
	Illustrated London News, (2 September 1848; 7 January, 4 February, 15 April, 24 June 1854; 28 January 1865)
	Llandudno Advertiser, (24 September 1896)

INDEX OF SHIPS

EXPLANATORY NOTES

Column 1. Name and Type of Ship
The following abbreviations are used in brackets after the name of each vessel to indicate its rig, motive power or function:

Bge	Barge	Frig	Frigate	Ship	Full rigged
Bq	Barque	Fy	Ferry	SlP	Sloop
Bqn	Barquentine	Gal	Galliot	Sink	Smack
Brig	Brig	Hulk	Hulk	Snow	Snow
Brtn	Brigantine	Ket	Ketch	Sr	Schooner
Cab	Cabin cruiser	LB	Lifeboat	SS	Steamship usually screw
Corv	Corvette	MB	Motorboat	Sub	Submarine
Cut	Cutter	MV	Motor vessel	Ur	Tanker
Cvel	Caravel	Pkt	Mail packet	Traw	Trawler
Dan	Dandy	Priv	Privateer	War	Warship
Dest	Destroyer	PS	Paddle steamer	Yawl	Yawl
Flat	Flat	Sail	Rig unknown	Yt	Yacht

Column 2: Home Port
The information given is intended only as a guide to the origin of a vessel. Where the information is available the actual home port is given, and this may have no link with the port of registration, eg, all ships built and operated from Porthmadog were registered a Caernarfon, and many Caernarfon-based vessels were registered at Liverpool. In some instances only the country of origin is given. Warships are listed by their respective navies, eg, Royal Navy.

Column 3: Fate
Some wrecks not named in the text of the book are listed in this index for record purposes. They can be recognised by the addition of a location in column 3; no location being given where there are page references for details to be found in the text. The term 'wreck' is used in its widest sense to include vessels put out of service by such mishaps as collision or bombing, or which had to appeal for salvage assistance due to storm damage or mechanical failure. The date of the wreck is given, preceded by one of the following code letters to indicate the type of mishap:

a	aground	e	mechanical failure	q	abandoned
b	bombed	f	fire wreck	s	sank
c	collided	h	holed	t	torpedoed
d	disappeared	m	mined	w	wrecked

Column 4: Page Reference
* Ships not mentioned in text but associated with incidents off the North Wales Coast.

SHIP	HOME PORT	FATE	PAGE REF.
A			
Abbey (Sr)	Beaumaris	s 1.2.1892	113
Abbotsford (SS)	Liverpool	w 19.7.1875 N Anglesey	72
Abermenai Ferry (Fy)	Caernarfon	s 1664, s 5.12.1785	85
Active (Sr)	Ipswich	w 5.12.1830	75
Active (Smk)		w 7.3.1835	75
Ada Mary (Ket)		w 27.3.1919	133
Adela (Smk)	Llandudno	s 1.1.1910 N of Great Orme	96
Admiral Moorsom (PS)	Holyhead	c 15.1.1885	65
Adroit (Sr)	Aberystwytb	w 20.7.1879 Porthdinllaen	34
Aeiger (SS)	Holland	a 1941	39
Aeron Belle (Sr)	Aberystwyth	s 20.2.1910 Abersoch	20
Agnes (Brig)		w 26.10.1859 Amlwch	72
Agnes (Flat)		s 1.2.1892	113
Albanian (SS)	Liverpool	c 1877 off Llandudno	111
Albion (Sr)	Beaumaris	h 12.2.1871 Bull Bay	72
Alert (Pkt)	Parkgate	w 26.3.1823	75
Alert (Smk)	Porthmadog	s 7.3.1858 Caernarfon Bay	34
Alert (Bq)	St John, NB	w 28.11.1897	66
Alexandra (SS)		w 9.2.1871 Clipera	58
Alfred H. Read (SS)	Liverpool	m 1917 Mersey approach	12
Alhambra (Bq)	Ireland	w 31.12.1845 Rhoscolyn	46
Alhambra (Bq)	Pillau	c 31.10.1883	63
Alice (Sr)	Liverpool	w 7.10.1850 Nimrod Rocks	58
Alice (Slp)	Conwy	s 26.l0.1859	99
Alice (Sr)	Nefyn	w 16.9.1873	127
Alice & Mary (Smk)	Bangor	w 25.1.1869	87
Alma (Sr)		w 26.10.1859	99
Alnwick (Sr)	Beaumaris	q 24.1.1895 St Patrick's Causeway	20
Alpha (Smk)	Pwllheli	s 13.11.1894 Pwllheli	20
Amalia (Bq)	Gothenborg	a 14.11.1896 Pwllheli	20
Amiaris (MB)	Bangor	a 9.1970 Glyn Garth	86
Amity (Smk)	Aberystwyth	s 11.8.1877 off Puffin Island	118
Amity (Slp)	Pwllheli	w 12.9.1891 Llandudno	96
Amlwch Packet (Sr)	Beaumaris	w 14.10.1881 Abererch	118
Amy (Flat)	Liverpool	w 28.8.1879 Hilbre Swash	12
Andrada (Bq)	Liverpool	w 24.3.1895 St Patrick's Causeway	20
Anglia (SS)	Holyhead	a 15.1.1922	68
Angloman (SS)	Liverpool	w 9.2.1897	80
Ann (Pkt)	Holyhead	d 9.1710	57
Ann (Frig)	Royal Navy	w 3.11.1760	33
Ann (Slp)	Aberdyfi	w 25.12.1836 Llangwnnadl	20
Ann (Flat)	Caernarfon	w 18.10.1858	30
Ann (Smk)	Conwy	s 21.10.1906 Cardigan Bay	20
Ann Alice (Sr)	Porthdinllaen	w 11.3.1877 Pt Lynas	72
Ann & Catherine (Smk)	Barmouth	s 25.7.1856 off Barmouth	20
Ann & Catherine (Sr)		s 11.12.1881 off Pt Lynas	72
Ann & Susan (Slp)	Bangor	w 9.12.1865 Amlwch	72
Anna Olga (Sr)	Russia	w Llandudno Bay	115
Anne (Smk)	Plymouth	w 5.12.1830	75
Anne (Brig)	Plymouth	w 15.9.1861 Holyhead	58
Annie (Sr)	Padstow	w 30.1.1877 St Tudwal Road	20
Annie Jones (Srnk)	Caernarfon	e 24.8.1894	34
Ann Jane (Sr)	Nefyn	w 27.12.1897 Cymryan Bay	46
Ann Margaret (Slp)	Conwy	w	102
Antares (MFV)	Poole	w 9.9.1972 Rhos-on-sea	
Apapa (SS)		m 28.11.1917	82
Aquila (SS)	Panama	e 23.10.1961 Nr Bardsey	20
Arabella (Fy)	Barmouth	w 1.8.1894	32
Archiduco Palatino (Brig)	Italy	w 1847	109
Arctic (SS)	New York	a 18.3.1854	78
Ardlough (MV)	Antigua	w 26.9.1988 Hoylake	*
Arethusa (Sr)	Caernarfon	w 18.3.1876 Caernarfon Bar	34
Arfestone (Ship)		w 1840 Hell's Mouth	20
Argo (MV)	Germany	a 27.4.1971 W. Hoyle	118
Aries (Yt)	Barrow	s 1880	63
Arion (Brig)	Germany	w 1850 Borthwen	34
Asmund (SS)	Norway	w 2.12.1930	68
Athabaska (Ship)	Liverpool	w 17.4.1838	120
Athena (Brig)	Candia	w 20.12.1852	49
Atlantic (Bq)	Boston	w 1.1868	51
Atlas (Slp)		w 11.1832	99
Auckland (Sail)	Dublin	a 22.2.1833	99
Avondale (SS)		w 9.12.1886	65
B			
Baltic (Sr)	Liverpool	w 10.1923 Beaumaris	86
Bangor (SS)	Beaumans	c 20.1.1915 with Cierbano off H'head	*

SHIP	HOME PORT	FATE	PAGE REF.	SHIP	HOME PORT	FATE	PAGE REF.
Charlotte (Brig)	Le Havre	2w 4.12.1855	27	**D**			
Charlotte (Sr)		w 3.1867		Dagmar (Bq)	Norway	w 9.12.1886	65
		Rhoscolyn	46	Dahomey (SS)	Liverpool	a 6.4.1898	66
Charlotte Ann (Sr)	Bangor	w 28.1.1887		Dakota (SS)	Liverpool	w 9.5.1877	
		Anglesey	*			E Mouse	76
Charming Jenny (Slp)		w 1715	45	Dalmatian (SS)	Liverpool	s 1872	30
Cherokee (Ship)		w 18.2.1854	126	Dasher (Sr)	Beaumaris	a 22.4.1868	
Chesterfield (Pkt)	Holyhead	s 1823				St Patrick's Causeway	20
		off Holyhead	58	Dee Ferry (Fy)	Queensferry	s 20. 12.1884	12
Christiana (SS)	Liverpool	h 1900	88			mid-river	
Cierbano (SS)	Spain	c20.1.1915		Deborah (Slp)	Pwllheli	w 3.7.1845	
		With Bangor off H'head	*			Great Orme	96
City of Durham (Bq)		a 3.2.1881		Denbighshire Lass (Sr)	Beaumaris	w 24. 1.1868	
		Porth Rbuffydd	46			Porthdinllaen	34
City of Halifax (Bq)	Liverpool	a 30. 1.1872		De Ruyter (MV)	Holland	a 10.1.1941	
		Llanaelhaiarn	34			Cymyran Bay	46
Clagan (Sr)	Barrow	w 28.6.1917	82	Dewi Wyn (Smk)	Porthmadog	s 1861	
Claudia (Slp)	Aberdyfi	w 25.10.1859				Cardigan Bay	20
		Aberdyfi	20	Diane (Cab)	Hoylake	w 27.8.1971	
Clermont (Pkt)	Parkgate	w 18.12.1790	59			W Hoyle	*
Clifton (Bq)	Liverpool	w 3.l.1876	51	Dido C (Ket)	Runcorn	a 1.1886	130
		Rhosneigr	72	Die Krone (Brig)	Prussia	w 26.12.1852	
Collina (Sr)	Porthdinllaen	w 8.3.1869				Caernarfon Bar	49
		Platters	74	Die Liebe (Gal)	Holland	w 1.1802	59
Columbia (Brtn)	Caernarfon	w 11.9.1866	34	Dirk Hattarick (Bq)	Waterford	w 1.1868	
		Porthdinllaen				Cymyran Bay	46
Columbian (SS)	Liverpool	a 18.9. 1890		Dobell (Smk)	Caernarfon	a 25.9.1911	
		Rhoscolyn	46			Barmouth Bar	20
Compeer (Sr)	Salcomhe	e 1.1l.1853		Dolphin (PS)		a 1.1843 Porthdinllaen	34
		off Cemlyn	76	Dora (Sr)	Chester	a 2.9.1897	
Confiance (Bq)	Liverpool	w 4. 12.1863				Conwy Bay	86
		Holyhead	58	Dora (Sr)	Porthmadog	s 10.9.1903	
Conflict (Ship)		a 1878 Rhosneigr	46			Abersoch	20
Connemara (SS)	Holyhead	c 23.6.1900		Dorothy & Mary (Sr)	Porthmadog	q 11.12.1883	
		c 20.3.1910	66			Holyhead	58
Conway, H.M.S. (Hulk)	Menai Strait	w 14.4.1953	89-94	Dorte Steen (MV)	Denmark	a 24.9.1972	
Conway's Pride (Slp)	Conwy	w 6.1897				Connahs Quay	*
		Llanddulas	118	Doudee (MBYt)	Conwy	f 29.8.1970	
Corsair (Bq)	Halifax, NS	w 27.l.1840				off Puffin Is	86
		Hoyle	118	Douglas Pennant (Sr)	Bangor	w 1868	
Cosmopolitan (Ship)	Liverpool	s 8.1848	49			Dulas Rocks	72
Cossack		s 11.11.1845	99	Douro (Sr)	Caernarfon	w 28.1.1873	
Countess of Caithness (Sr)	Gloucester	h 2.1884	58			Pt Lynas	72
		Holyhead		Dove (Sr)	Abersoch	w 13.1.1847	20
Cufic (SS)	Liverpool	q 20.12.1900	80	Dove (Slp)	Pwllheli	w 1869	51
Culloden (Ship)	Liverpool	w 9.12.1854	27	Dreadnought (Sr)	Barmouth	w 14.10. 1881	
Curlew (Smk)	Conwy	s 18.8.1898	113			Abererch	20
Cyclops (Hulk)	Royal Navy	q 24.3.1947	53	Dronning Sophie (Bq)	Norway	a 7.10.1889	
Cygnet (Slp)	Nefyn	w 12.5.1870 Pt				Rhoscolyn	46
		Lynas	72	Duchess of Gloucester (Sail)		w 26.10.1859	99
Cymraes (Flat)	Beaumaris	w 25.1.1861		Duchess of Sutherland (PS)	Holyhead	c 8.9.1875	63
		Penmon	86	Dunchoo (Ship)		w 1814	
Cymro (Smk)		w 7.12.1866	111			Porth Colmon	20
Cyprian (SS)	Liverpool	w 14.10.1881	38	Dundalk (SS)		t 14.10.1918	
						5m NW of Skerries	58
				Dundarg (Sr)		s 1920 Llandudno	96
				Dusty Miller (Bq)	Caernarfon	a 10.10.1878	30

SHIP	HOME PORT	FATE	PAGE REF.	SHIP	HOME PORT	FATE	PAGE REF.
Jane & Ann (Sr)	Caernarfon	w 14.5.1879		John O' Gaunt (Ship)	London	w 16.1.1854	49
		Porthdinllaen	34	John Parry (Sr)	Bangor	w 9.12.1901	82
Jane & Ann (Slp)	Liverpool	w 1885		John Welsh (Sail)	Savanilla	w 29.7.1836	120
		Red Wharf Bay	72	Jolly Charles (SS)		a	103
Jane & Ann (Sr)	Caernarfon	s 10.12.1919		Joseph (Sail)	Liverpool	w 26.10.1859	99
		Porthdinllaen	34	Joseph (Slp)	Pwllheli	w 1.10.1891	
Jane & Ann (Sr)	Caernarfon	w 10.1.1920				Abersoch	20
		Penmon	86	Joseph Nicholson (Sr)	Nefyn	w 1898	
Jane & Annie (Sr)	Caernarfon	w 1902				Hell's Mouth	20
		Hell's Mouth	20	Joseph W (MB)	Traeth Baychan	s 20.9.1971	
Jane & Betty (Slp)	Conwy	w 3.1836				Point Lynas	72
		nr Holyhead	58	Jubilee (Sr)	Preston	w 22. 12.1886	
Jane & Catherine (Flat)	Conwy	s 1867				Penmon	86
		Cardigan Bay	20	Julia (Sr)	Gloucester	q 21.12.1900	
Jane & Eliza (Sr)	Pwllheli	w 19.10.1885	30			off Holyhead	58
Jane & Ellen (Sr)	Bangor	w 11.11.1877	20	Julia (Sr)	Runcorn	s 23.3.1905	
		Abersoch				Porthdinllaen	34
Jane & Margaret (Ship)	Liverpool	d 6.2.1837	120	June Starfish (Traw)	Rhyl	s 11.6.1994	
Jane & Mary (Slp)	Caernarfon	w 29.8.1869	127			off Rhyl	144
Jane & Sarah (Smk)	Wicklow	w 8.1 .185	2	Juno (Bq)	Russia	w 27.12.1852	49
		Hoylake	12	Juno (Yawl)	Beaumaris	w 7.12.1884	
Jane Douglas (Sr)	Banff	w 17.11.1893				Penmon	86
		Holyhead	58	Jura (SS)	Liverpool	w 3.11.1864	
Jane Ellen (Sr)	Porthmadog	w 4.10.1881				W Hoyle	118
		Ahererch	20	J. W. Wearing (Sr)	Lancaster	w 8.12.1901	53
Jane Tudor (Bq)	Bath, Maine	a 15.2.1847	109				
Janet & Alice (Sr)	Porthmadog	s 26.11.1884		**K**			
		Cardigan Bay	*	Kate (Sr)	Amlwch	f 31.1.1933	82
Jenny Jones (Smk)	Barmouth	s 24.3. 1866	34	Kendal Castle (Sr)	Amlwch	w 26.10.1859	72
		Porthdinllaen				Amlwch	
JMK (Sr)	Dublin	w 3.12.1903		Kenilworth (Ship)	Liverpool	w 14.1.1870	29
		Penmon	86	Kimya (MV)	Malta	s 6.1.1991	
Johara (Slp)	Holyhead	a 16.8.1970				off H'head	20
		Holyhead	58	Kingfisher (SS)	New York	a 9.8.1940	
John (Sail)	St Malo	a 1590				Abersoch	
		Pwllheli	20	King George (Pkt)	Parkgate	w 8.1806	120
John & Ann (Slp)	Nefyn	s 22.12.1880		King Ja-Ja (SS)	Liverpool	q 24.12.1877	111
		Cemaes	72			Llandudno	
John & Eliza (Smk)	Beaumaris	q 3.1.1877		Kirkmichael (Bq)		w 22.12.1894	
		Holyhead	58			Holyhead	67
John & Henry (Sr)	Runcorn	s 10.1.1903		Kirkwynd (SS)	Glasgow	a 12.7.1926	
		Porthdinllaen	34			Rhoscolyn	122
John & Jennifer (Sr)	Fowey	a 1.1.1874	58	Knut (SS)	Holland	m 1941	39
John & Margaret (Sr)	Portlimadog	w 1912		Kohinoor (Sr)	Aberdyfi	s 4.12.1890	20
		Lianbedrog	*			Cardigan Bay	
John & Robert (Sr)	Nefyn	q 20.5.1887		Kragero (Bq)	Norway	a 2.8.1895	
		Porthdinllaen	34			St Patrick's Causeway	20
John Bagshaw (Brig)		w 2.1870		Kyle Firth (SS)	Glasgow	w 13.5.1940	55
		nr Llanddwyn	51	Kyle Prince (SS)	Liverpool	w 8.10.1938	55
John Bannerman (Ship)	St. John	w 3.3.1855					
		Holy Island	61/69	**L**			
John Gibson (Sr)	Fleetwood	w 8.10.1896		Lady Agnes (Sr)	Newquay	w 8.10.1896	102
		Abersoch	20	Lady Charlotte Guest (Sr)	Cardiff	e 31.10.1843	48
John G. Walter (Sr)	Nova Scotia	a 9.3.1918	32	Lady Fielding (Sr)	Amlwch	w 16.9.1908	
John Herbert	Caernarfon	s 10.1891(?)				Penmon	86
		Moelfre	72	Lady Harriet (Sail)	Llandudno	s 1847	111
John Nelson (Sail)	Beaumaris	s 1.2.1892	113	Lady Hincks (Ship)	Liverpool	w 12.12.1883	
						Trefor	39

SHIP	HOME PORT	FATE	PAGE REF.	SHIP	HOME PORT	FATE	PAGE REF.
Martha (Sr)	Porthdinllaen	w 27.9.1875 Pistyll	54	*Mermaid* (Slp)	Pwllheli	s 1849 Bardsey Sound	20
Mary (Yt)	Royal Navy	w 25.3.1675	71	*Mersey* (Sr)	Beaumaris	a 7.1.1878 Amlwch	72
Mary (Brtn)	Caernarfon	w 26.4.1792	120				
Mary (Slp)	Wicklow	s 22.l0.1834 off Holyhead	58	*Mersey* (SS)	Liverpool	w 22.6.1394	53
				Messenger	Caernarfon	w 26.10.1859	99
Mary (Slp)	Waterford	w 25.10.1834	87	*Meteor Flag* (Brtn)	Londonderry	w 10.1870 Caernarfon Bar	34
Mary (Flat)	Ipswich	w 9.1.1852 Bangor	128				
Mary (Sail)	Amlwch	f 3.1862	99	*Michael Wickham* (Smk)		s 29.10.1843 off Holyhead	58
Mary & Elizabeth (Sr)	Pwllheli	w 14.1.1843	25				
Mary & Martha (Sr)	Chester	q 5.10.1891 off Holyhead	58	*Midsummer* (Smk)	Douglas	w 28.11.1903 off Llanddwyn	46
Mary Ann (Slp)	Pwllheli	w 1852 Prestatyn	118	*Milborne* (MV)	Poole	a 20.3.1953 Rhoscolyn	46
Mary Ann (Sail)	Liverpool	w 31.12.1856 Rhyl	118	*Millie Bain* (Brtn)	Teignmouth	s 2.1.1899 off Holyhead	58
Mary Ann (Sr)	Faversham	w 10.1923 Dutchman's Bank	81	*Millom Castle* (Ket)	Barrow	e 1924 & 25 off Abersoch	20
Mary Ann Lewis (Sr)		w 10.1843 Porthdinllaen	34	*Minde* (Bq)	Farsund	s 11.10.1896 Penmon	86
Mary Catherine (Sip)	Caernarfon	w 18.1.1820	120	*Minerva* (SS)	Cork	w 8.1854	78
Mary Coles (Sr)	Port Dinorwic	w 5.5.1882 Point Lynas	72	*Miss Beck* (Sr)	Caernarfon	q 18.1.1881 Porthdinllaen	34
Mary Elizabeth (Sr)	Pwllheli	w 30.11.1867 nr Holyhead	*	*Missouri* (SS)	Liverpool	w 1.3.1886 P'-y Post	53
Mary Grace (Smk)	Bangor	c 24.8.1874	87	*M. J. Hedley* (SS)		a 13.1.1905 N Stack	58
Mary Jane (Sr)	Liverpool	q 22.9.1874 off Holyhead	58	*Moana Lua* (Cab)	Llandudno	w 24.7.1970 Craigydon	96
Mary Jane (Sr)	Lancaster	w 8.9.1908 Dutchman's Bank	86	*Modwen* (Yt)	Moelfre	w 1900	82
Mary Lord		w 29.10.1911 Beaumaris	86	*Moel-y-don-Ferry* (Fy)	Llanidan	w 6.10.1710	85
				Mona (Smk)	Bangor	w 2.12.1883 N of Prestatyn	118
Mary Reynolds (Sr)	Nefyn	w 26.9.1875 Caernarfon Bar	34				
Mary Roberts (Sr)	Nefyn	w 12.11.1879 Porthdinllaen	34	*Monk* (PS)	Caernarfon	w 7.1.1843	36
				Monktown (Sr)	Liverpool	q 22.9.1874 off Holyhead	58
Mary Scott (Ship)	Liverpool	c 9.5.1841 Liverpool Bay	118	*Montana* (SS)	Liverpool	w 14.3.1880 N Anglesey	72
Matilda (Brig)	Plymouth	w 26.6.1853 S Stack	27	*Montreal* (SS)	Liverpool	c 29.1.1918 Irish Sea	*
Matje (SS)	Hull	a 29.10.1927 Porthdinllaen	111	*Morning Star* (Sr)	Caernarfon	s 7.2.1866 Llandudno	96
Maude (Yt)	Glasgow	s 6.8.1904 Penmon	86	*Mountaineer* (Ship)	Liverpool	w 18.10.1841	48
Mayflower (Slp)	Caernarfon	w 7.1862 Puffin Is	86	*Mouse* (Sr)	Cardigan	w 7.10.1896 Abersoch	20
Mayflower (SS)	Liverpool	w 25.10.1949 Salt Is	55	*Mrs Assheton Smith*	Caernarfon	d 12.1866 out of Caernarfon	*
May Queen (Ship)	Liverpool	w 1.1868 Barmouth	29	*My Mink* (Cab)	- -	s 7.7.1963 Dee Estuary	*
Meath (SS)	Sunderland	w 1.2.1892	66	**N**			
Medoc (Bq)	Bordeaux	w 19.11.1869	29	*Nafsiporos* (MV)	Greece	e 2.12.1966	84
Melantho (Brig)	Whitby	w 16.11.1824 Llanddwyn	*	*Nanny* (Brig)	Porthdinllaen	w 1803 Porthdinllaen	34
Melwood (Cab)	Rhyl	a 3.5.1973 Llandudno	*	*Napier Star* (SS)	London	c 18.8.1935	140
				Neptune (Ship)		s 1825	23
Merlin (Sr)	Llanelly	c 17.10.1875	63	*Newry* (Ship)	Ireland	w 16.4.1830	36

SHIP	HOME PORT	FATE	PAGE REF.	SHIP	HOME PORT	FATE	PAGE REF.
Stewart (Bq)	Liverpool	w 6.4.1901 PorthColmon	22	*Titania* (Bq)		w 22.12.1894 Holyhead	58
Stockton (Dest)	US Navy	c 30.3.1918	68	*Tivy Lass*	Newport	a 27.12.1852 Llanddwyn	46
Strathmore (Brig)	Leith	w 4.1841 Trefor	34	*Topaz* (Smk)	Milford	s 8.10.1896 Abersoch	20
St. Tudno (Mv)	Liverpool	a 1946 Beaumaris, refloated	132	*Town of Wexford* (SS)	Wexford	w 4.1.1852	61
Success (Slp)	Aberdyfi	e 26.10.1859	99	*Trafalgar* (Sr)		w late 1830 SW Mouse	72
Sumatra (MV)	Holland	b 5.ll.1941	72	*Transit*	Boston	w 1839 Hell's Mouth	20
Sunbeam (MB)	Llandudno	w 3.7.1968 Little Orme	96	*Trebiskin* (Ket)	Cornwall	w 23.12.1901 Rhoscolyn	46
Sunbury (Snow)	New Orleans	w approx 1835 Aberffraw	47	*Trefriw Trader* (Flat)	Conwy	s 29.4.1849	75
Supply (Slp)	Pwllheli	w 1838	99	*Trevor* (Pkt)	Parkgate	w 19.10.1775	120
Supply (Sr)	Bristol	a 25.8.1877 Dutchman's Bank	86	*Troy* (Ship)	Boston	h 19.11.1859	29
Supply (man o'war)	Royal Navy	w 11.1.1690 Hoylake	*	*Tryfan* (Flat)		w 1932 N of Beaumaris	86
Susan (Brig)	London	w 29.11.1833	87	*Turkestan* (Ship)	Liverpool	w 18.2.1876 Harlech	20
Swallow (Brig)		a 1.9.1829 Dinas Dinlle	??	*Turtle Dove* (Sr)	Caernarfon	w 12.10.1870 Great Orme	111
Swallow (Slp)	Pwllheli	w 1863 Abersoch	20	*Twelve Apostles* (Sr)	Pwllheli	w 23. 11.1898	31
Sylph (Sr)	Newquay,	w 26.10.1859 Cardiganshire	99	*Two Brothers* (Cut)	Liverpool	w 11.1770	120
Syren (Ket)	Beaumaris	s 8.3.1908 Pwllheli	20	*Two Brothers* (Smk)	Pwllheli	w 10.9.1903 Pwllheli	20
				Two Brothers (Sr)	Nefyn	w 16.3.1907 Abersoch	20
T							
Taliesin (Tug)		a 26.8.1897 W Llandudno	86	**U**			
Tal-y-fan (SS)	Liverpool	w 14.10.1881 Porthdinllaen	43	*U-87* (Sub)	German Navy	s 25.12.1917 off Lleyn	20
Talyfoel Ferry (Fy)	Caernarfon	s 13.4.1723	85	*U-242* (Sub)	German Navy	s 30.4.1945	83
Talyfoel Ferry (Fy)	Caernarfon	s 5.12.1820	86	*U-325* (Sub)	German Navy	s 30.4.1945	83
Taki (Yt)		q 27.10.1862 Fairbourne	*	*U-1024* (Sub)	German Navy	s 12.4.1945	83
Tartar (Bq)		w 1850 Caernarfon Bar	20	*Una* (Sr)	Porthmadog	w 28.2.1881 Skerries	72
Telegraph (SS)	Holyhead	a 17.4.1863	62	*Uncle Tom* (Flat)	Runcorn	w 13.9.1861	111
Temperance (Sr)	Belfast	q 1.1857 Rhyl	118	*Undaunted* (Sr)	Plymouth	w 7.11.1890 Penmon	86
Temperance (Sr)	Llanhedrog	w 23.8.1868 Aberdyfi	20	*Union* (Sr)	Conwy	s 5.12.1852 Holyhead	58
Temple (Sail)		s 21.5.1852 Holyhead	58	*Unity* (Sr)	Beaumaris	c 14.12.1909 Penrhyndu	20
Tenby Castle (Bq)	Liverpool	w 17.12.1889	65	*Urgent* (Bq)	Liverpool	w 17.11.1844 nr Llanddwyn	46
The Brothers	Liverpool	w 2.1802	59				
Thetis (Sr)	Pwllheli	e 7.8.1880 Porthdinllaen	34	**V**			
Thetis (Sub)	Royal Navy	s 1.6.1939	133	*VA-3* (hovercraft)	Rhyl-Hoylake	w 17.9.1962	138
Thomas (Sr)	Nefyn	s 1857 Holyhead Bay	58	*Valhalla* (Brtn)	Farsund	w 22.12.1894 Holyhead	58
Thomas & Ann (Slp)	Bangor	w 5.12.1876	127	*Vans Sans Peur* (Traw)	Brittany	a 25.3.1948	32
Thomas Humphreys (Bq)	Norway	w 12.1.1867 *Cemlyn*	*	*Vapella* (Bq)	New Orleans	w 24.2.1868	29
Three Susans (Brig)	Bangor	w 12.1863 Porthdinllaen	34	*Varchwel* (Slp)	Caerhun	w 10.1844	99
Timbo (SS)	Whitby	a 3.12.1920	54	*Vella* (Ship)	Spain	w 26.10.1859 Porth Colmon	26

INDEX OF OTHER VESSELS NAMED IN THE TEXT

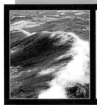

INDEX

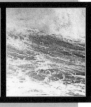

The remains of a 19th century shipwreck which lay for many years outside the Min-y-don Hotel, Red Wharf Bay.

LOST BUT NOT FORGOTTEN
THE FISHING VESSEL
· KATY ·
LEFT CONWY 16th JANUARY 1994.
CREW MEMBERS
L.S. ROWLANDS-ROBERTS (SAM)
AGED 22.
G. HUGHES (COCHYN)
AGED 30.
R. HALL (ROBBO)
AGED 20.